The Life, History, and Travels of Kah-Ge-Ga-Gah-Bowh

The Life, History, and Travels of Kah-Ge-Ga-Gah-Bowh

George Copway

MINT EDITIONS

The Life, History, and Travels of Kah-Ge-Ga-Gah-Bowh was first published in 1847.

This edition published by Mint Editions 2021.

ISBN 9781513283425 | E-ISBN 9781513288444

Published by Mint Editions®

MINT
EDITIONS

minteditionbooks.com

Publishing Director: Jennifer Newens
Design & Production: Rachel Lopez Metzger
Project Manager: Micaela Clark
Typesetting: Westchester Publishing Services

CONTENTS

A Word to the Reader

I t would be presumptuous in one, who has but recently been brought out of a wild and savage state; and who has since received but three years' schooling, to undertake, without any assistance, to publish to the world a work of any kind. It is but a few years since I began to speak the English language. An unexpected opportunity occurred of submitting my manuscript to a friend, who has kindly corrected all *serious* grammatical errors, leaving the unimportant ones wholly untouched, that my own style may be exhibited as truly as possible. The public, the printers, and myself, are indebted to him for his kind aid, and he has my most sincere thanks. The Printers, also, will accept my hearty thanks for their kind indulgence in affording me every facility in their power, in bringing out the work in so short a time, and for 'getting it up' with so much neatness. The language (except in a few short sentences), the plan, and the arrangement are all my own; and I am wholly responsible for all the statements, and the remaining defects. My work is now accomplished; and I am too well aware of the many faults which are still to be found therein. Little could I imagine, that I should have to contend with so many obstacles. All along, have I felt my great deficiency; and my inadequacy for such an undertaking. I would fain hope, however, that the kind Reader will throw the mantle of charity over errors of every kind. I am a stranger in a strange land! And often, when the sun is sinking in the western sky, I think of my former home; my heart yearns for the loved of other days, and tears flow like the summer rain. How the heart of the wanderer and pilgrim, after long years of absence, beats, and his eyes fill, as he catches a glance at the hills of his nativity, and reflects upon the time when he pressed the lips of a Mother, or Sister, now cold in death. Should I live, this painful pleasure will yet be mine. *Blessed be the Lord, who hath helped me hitherto."*

KAH-GE-GA-GAH-BOWH,
ALIAS
GEORGE COPWAY.

ALBANY, JANUARY, 1847.

Preface

I n presenting my life to the public, I do so with the greatest diffidence, and at the earnest solicitation of numerous friends. I am an Indian, and am well aware of the difficulties I have to encounter to win the favorable notice of the white man. Yet one great object prompts me to persevere, and that is, that I may, in connection with my life, present the *present state* and *prospects* of my poor countrymen—feeling that the friends of humanity may still labor and direct their benevolence to those who were once the lords of the land on which the white man lives—and assist in rescuing them from an untimely and unchristian grave.

I have noticed some of our prominent chiefs now living; the missionaries laboring amongst my people; the extent of the missionary field; and an appeal to all who feel interested in the welfare of the Indian race.

If ever I see the day when my people shall become happy and prosperous, I shall then feel great and lasting pleasure, which will more than repay me for the pain, both of body and mind, which I have endured for the last twelve years. My motto is—*"My poor People."*

In all my crooked paths, I have endeavored to mean well. I thank my friends for their kind gifts and wishes. Yet still as much, and more, remains to be accomplished.

Pray for us—that *religion* and *science* may lead us on to intelligence and virtue; that we may imitate the good white man, who, like the eagle, builds its nest on the top of some high rock—*science;* that we may educate our children, and turn their minds to God. Help us, O help us to live—and teach us to die a christian's death, that our spirits may mingle with the blessed above.

KAH-GE-GA-GAH-BOWH

I

The Christian will no doubt feel for my poor people, when he hears the story of one brought from that unfortunate race called the Indians. The lover of humanity will be glad to see that that once powerful race can be made to enjoy the blessings of life.

What was once impossible—or rather thought to be—is made possible through my experience. I have made many close observations of men, and things around me; but, I regret to say, that I do not think I have made as good use of my opportunities as I might have done. It will be seen that I know but little—yet O how precious *that little!*—I would rather loose my right hand than be deprived of it.

I loved the woods, and the chase. I had the nature for it, and gloried in nothing else. The mind for letters was in me, *but was asleep,* till the dawn of Christianity arose, and awoke the slumbers of the soul into energy and action.

You will see that I served the imaginary gods of my poor blind father. I was out early and late in quest of the favors of the *Mon-e-doos* (spirits), who, it was said, were numerous—who filled the air! At early dawn I watched the rising of the *palace* of the Great Spirit—*the sun*—who, it was said, made the world!

Early as I can recollect, I was taught that it was the gift of the many spirits to be a good hunter and warrior; and much of my time I devoted in search of their favors. On the mountain top, or along the valley, or the water brook, I searched for some kind intimation from the spirits who made their residence in the noise of the water falls.

I dreaded to hear the voice of the angry spirit in the gathering clouds. I looked with anxiety to catch a glimpse of the wings of the Great Spirit, who shrouded himself in rolling white and dark clouds—who, with his wings, fanned the earth, and laid low the tall pines and hemlock in his course—who rode in whirlwinds and tornadoes, and plucked the trees from their woven roots—who chased other gods from his course—who drove the Bad Spirit from the surface of the earth, down to the dark caverns of the deep. Yet he was a kind spirit. My father taught me to call that spirit Ke-sha-mon-e-doo—*Benevolent spirit*—for his ancestors taught him no other name to give to that spirit who made the earth, with all its variety and smiling beauty. His benevolence I saw in the running of the streams, for the animals to quench their thirst and the fishes to live; the fruit of the earth teemed wherever I looked. Every thing I saw smilingly said Ke-sha-mon-e-doo nin-ge-oo-she-ig—*the Benevolent spirit made me.*

Where is he? My father pointed to the sun. What is his will concerning me, and the rest of the Indian race? This was a question that I found no one could answer, until a beam from heaven shone on my pathway, which was very dark, when first I saw that there was a true heaven—not in the far-setting sun, where the Indian anticipated a rest, a home for his spirit—but in the bosom of the Highest.

I view my life like the mariner on the wide ocean, without a compass, in the dark night, as he watches the heavens for the north star, which his eye having discovered, he makes his way amidst surging seas, and tossed by angry billows into the very jaws of death, till he arrives safely anchored at port. I have been tossed with hope and fear in this life; no star-light shone on my way, until the men of God pointed me to a Star in the East, as it arose with all its splendor and glory. It was the Star of Bethlehem. I could now say in the language of the poet—

> *"Once on the raging seas I rode,*
> *The storm was loud, the night was dark;*
> *The ocean yawned, and rudely blowed*
> *The wind that tossed my foundered bark."*

Yes, I hope to sing some day in the realms of bliss—

> *"It was my guide, my light, my all!*
> *It bade my dark foreboding cease;*
> *And through the storms and danger's thrawl,*
> *It led me to the port of peace."*

I have not the happiness of being able to refer to written records in narrating the history of my forefathers; but I can reveal to the world what has long been laid up in my memory; so that when "I go the way of all the earth," the crooked and singular paths which I have made in the world, may not only be a warning to others, but may inspire them with a trust in God. And not only a warning and a trust, but also that the world d may learn that there once lived such a man as Kah-ge-ga-gah-bowh, when they read his griefs and his joys.

My parents were of the Ojebwa nation, who lived on the lake back of Cobourg, on the shores of Lake Ontario, Canada West. The lake called Rice Lake, where there was a great quantity of wild rice, and much game of different kinds, before the whites cleared away the woods, where the deer and the bear then resorted.

My father and mother were taught the religion of their nation. My father became a medicine man in the early part of his life, and always had by him the implements of war, which generally distinguish our head men. He was as good a hunter as any in the tribe. Very few brought more furs than he did in the spring. Every spring they returned from their hunting grounds. The Ojebwas each claimed, and claim to this day, hunting grounds, rivers, lakes, and whole districts of country. No one hunted on each other's ground. My father had the northern fork of the river Trent, above Bellmont lake.

My great-grandfather was the first who ventured to settle at Rice Lake, after the Ojebwa nation defeated the Hurons, who once inhabited all the lakes in Western Canada, and who had a large village just on the top of the hill of the Anderson farm, (which was afterwards occupied by the Ojebwas,) and which furnished a magnificent view of the lakes and surrounding country. He was of the *Crane tribe*, i.e. had a crane for his to-tem—*coat of arms*—which now forms the totem of the villagers, excepting those who have since come amongst us from other villages by intermarriage, for there was a law that no one was to marry one of the same totem, for all considered each other as being related. He must have been a daring adventurer—a *warrior*—for no one would have ventured to go and settle down on the land from which they had just driven the Hurons, whom the Ojebwas conquered and reduced, unless he was a great hero. It is said that he lived about the islands of Rice Lake, secreting himself from the enemy for several years, until some others came and joined him, when they formed a settlement on one of the islands. He must have been a great hunter, for this was one of the principal inducements that made him venture there, for there must have been abundance of game of every kind. The Ojebwas are called, here and all around, Massissaugays, because they came from Me-sey Sah-gieng, at the head of Lake Huron, as you go up to Sault St. Marie falls.

Here he lived in jeopardy—with his life in his hand—enduring the unpleasant idea that he lived in the land of bones—*amidst the gloom*, which shrouded the once happy and populous village of the Hurons; here their bones lay broadcast around his wigwam; where, among these woods once rang the war cry of the Hurons, echoing along the valley of the river Trent, but whose sinewed arms now laid low, with their badges and arms of war, in one common grave, near the residence of Peter Anderson, Esq. Their graves, forming a hillock, are now all that remain of this once powerful nation. Their bones, gun barrels, tomahawks, war spears, large scalping knives, are yet to be found there. This must have taken place soon after the formation of the settlement in Quebec.

The *Crane tribe* became the sole proprietors of this part of the Ojebwa land; the descendants of this tribe will continue to wear the distinguishing sign; except in a few instances, the chiefs are of this tribe.

My grandfather lived here about this time, and held some friendly intercourse with the whites. My father here learned the manners, customs, and worship of the nation. He, and others, became acquainted with the early settlers, and have ever been friendly with the whites. And I know the the day when he used to shake the hand of the white man, and, *very friendly,* the white man would say, "*take some whiskey.*" When he saw any hungering for venison, he gave them to eat; and some, in return for his kindness, have repaid him after they became good and great farmers.

My mother was of the *Eagle tribe;* she was a sensible woman; she was as good a hunter as any of the Indians; she could shoot the deer, and the ducks flying, as well as they. Nature had done a great deal for her, for she was active; and she was much more cleanly than the majority of our women in those days. She lived to see the day when most of her children were given up to the Lord in christian baptism; while she experienced a change of heart, and the fullness of God in man, for she lived daily in the enjoyment of God's favors. I will speak more of her at a proper time, respecting her life and happy death.

My father still lives; he is from sixty-five to seventy years old, and is one of the chiefs of Rice Lake Indian Village. He used to love fire-water before he was converted to God, but now lives in the enjoyment of religion, and he is happy without the devil's spittle—*whiskey.* If christianity had not come, and the grace of God had not taken possession of his heart, his head would soon have been laid low beneath the fallen leaves of the forest, and I, left, in my youthful days, an orphan. But to God be all the praise for his timely deliverance.

The reader will see that I cannot boast of an exalted parentage, nor trace the past history to some renowned warrior in days of yore, but let

GEORGE COPWAY

the above suffice. My fathers were those who endured much; who first took possession of the conquered lands of the Hurons.

I was born in *nature's wide domain!* The trees were all that sheltered my infant limbs—the blue heavens all that covered me. I am one of nature's children; I have always admired her; she shall be my glory; her features—her robes, and the wreath about her brow—the seasons—her stately oaks, and the evergreen—her hair—ringlets over the earth, all contribute to my enduring love of her; and wherever I see her, emotions of pleasure roll in my breast, and swell and burst like waves on the shores of the ocean, in prayer and praise to Him, who has placed me in her hand. It is thought great to be born in palaces, surrounded with wealth—but to be born in nature's wide domain is greater still!

I was born sometime in the fall of 1818, near the mouth of the river Trent, called in our language, Sah-ge-dah-we-ge-wah-noong, while my father and mother were attending the annual distribution of the presents from the government to the Indians. I was the third of our family; a brother and sister being older, both of whom died. My brother died without the knowledge of the Saviour, but my sister experienced the power of the loving grace of God. One brother, and two step-brothers, are still alive.

I remember the tall trees, and the dark woods—the swamp just by, where the little wren sang so melodiously after the going down of the sun in the west—the current of the broad river Trent—the skipping of the fish, and the noise of the rapids a little above. It was here I first saw the light; a little fallen-down shelter, made of evergreens, and a few dead embers, the remains of the last fire that shed its genial warmth around, were all that marked the spot. When I last visited it, nothing but fur poles stuck in the ground, and they were leaning on account of decay. Is this dear spot, made green by the tears of memory, any less enticing and hallowed than the palaces where princes are born? I would much more glory in this birth-place, with the broad canopy of heaven above me, and the giant arms of the forest trees for my shelter, than to be born in palaces of marble, studded with pillars of gold! Nature will be nature still, while palaces shall decay and fall in ruins. Yes, Niagara will be Niagara a thousand years hence! the rainbow, a wreath over her brow, shall continue as long as the sun, and the flowing of the river! While the work of art, however impregnable, shall in atoms fall.

Our wigwam we always carried with us wherever we went. It was made in the following manner: Poles were cut about fifteen feet long;

three with crotches at the end, which were stuck in the ground some distance apart, the upper ends meeting, and fastened with bark; and then other poles were cut in circular form and bound round the first, and then covered with plaited reeds, or sewed birch bark, leaving an opening on top for the smoke to escape. The skins of animals formed a covering for a gap, which answered for a door. The family all seated tailor-fashion on mats. In the fall and winter they were generally made more secure, for the purpose of keeping out the rain and cold. The covering of our wigwam was always carried by my mother, whenever we went through the woods. In the summer it was easier and pleasanter to move about from place to place, than in the winter. In the summer we had birch bark canoes, and with these we traveled very rapidly and easily. In the winter every thing was carried upon the back. I have known some Indians to carry a whole deer—not a small one, but a buck. If an Indian could lift up his pack off the ground by means of his arms, it was a good load, not too light nor too heavy. I once carried one hundred and ninety-six weight of flour, twelve pounds of shot, five pounds of coffee, and some sugar, about a quarter of a mile, without resting—the flour was in two bags. It felt very heavy. This was since I traveled with the missionaries, in going over one of the portages in the west.

Our summer houses were made like those in gardens among the whites, except that the skeleton is covered with bark.

The hunting grounds of the Indians were secured by right, a law and custom among themselves. No one was allowed to hunt on another's land, without invitation or permission. If any person was found trespassing on the ground of another, all his things were taken from him, except a hand full of shot, powder sufficient to serve him in going *straight* home, a gun, a tomahawk, and a knife; all the fur, and other things, were taken from him. If he were found a second time trespassing, all his things were taken away from him, except food sufficient to subsist on while going home. And should he still come a third time to trespass on the same, or another man's hunting grounds, his nation, or tribe, are then informed of it, who take up his case. If still he disobey, he is banished from his tribe.

My father's hunting ground was at the head of Crow River, a branch of the River Trent, north of the Prince Edward District, Canada West. There are two branches to this river—one belongs to George Poudash, one of the principal chiefs of our nation; the other to my father; and the Crow River belongs to another chief by the name of John Crow. During the last war the Indians did not hunt or fish much for nearly six years, and at the end of that time there were large quantities of beaver, otter, minks, lynx, fishes, &c.

These hunting grounds abound with rivers and lakes; the face of the country is swampy and rocky; the deer and the bear abound in these woods; part of the surrendered territory is included in it. In the year 1818, 1,800,000 acres of it were surrendered to the British government. For how much, do you ask? For $2,960 per annum! What a *great sum* for British generosity!

Much of the back country still remains unsold, and I hope the scales will be removed from the eyes of my poor countrymen, that they may see the robberies perpetrated upon them, before they surrender another foot of territory.

From these lakes and rivers come the best furs that are caught in Western Canada. Buyers of fur get large quantities from here. They are then shipped to New-York city, or to England. Whenever fruit is plenty, bears are also plenty, and there is much bear hunting. Before the whites came amongst us, the skins of these animals served for clothing; they are now sold from three to eight dollars a piece.

My father generally took one or two families with him when he went to hunt; all were to hunt, and place their gains into one common stock till spring (for they were often out all winter), when a division took place.

II

I n the fall we gathered the wild rice, and in the winter we were in the interior. Some winters we suffered most severely, on account of the depth of snow, and the cold; our wigwams were often buried in snow. We not only suffered from the snow and the cold, but from hunger. Our party would be unable to hunt, and being far from the white settlements, we were often in want of food. I will narrate a circumstance of our sufferings, when I come to speak of the actual condition of our people, before christianity was introduced among us, which, when I think of it, I can not but bless God for his preserving kindness to us, in sparing us to hear his blessed word.

Soon after being christianized, my father and another Indian, by the name of Big John, and myself, went out hunting; my father left his family near the mission station, living in the wigwam. While we were out on the hunting grounds, we found out that some Indians had gone before us on the route up the river, and every day we gained upon them; their tracks were fresh. The river and the lakes were frozen, and we had to walk on the ice. For some days together we did not fire a gun, for fear they would hear it and go from us, where we could not find them. At length we found them by the banks of the river; they were Nah-doo-ways or Mohawks, from Bay Quinty; there were seven of them, tall fellows. We shook hands with them; they received us kindly. My father had determined to take all they had, if we should overtake them. After they gave us a good dinner of boiled beaver, my father stepped across the fire and ripped open two packs of beaver furs, that were just by him. He said to them "We have only one custom among us, and that is well known to all; this river, and all that is in it are mine; I have come up the river behind you, and you appear to have killed all before you. This is mine, and this is is mine," he said, as he touched with the handle of his tomahawk each of the packs of beaver, otter, and muskrat skins. I expected every moment to see my father knocked down with a tomahawk, but none dared touch him; he counted the skins and then threw them across the fire-place to us. After this was done, the same thing took place with the guns; only one was left them to use on their way home. He talked to them by signs, and bade them, as the sailors say, "weigh anchor and soon be under way"; they left, and we took possession of the temporary wigwam they had built. We never saw them afterwards on our hunting grounds, though some of them have been there since.

My father was ever kind and affectionate to me, particularly after the death of my brother, which was occasioned by the going off of a gun, the load passing through the arm and so fractured it that it soon mortified and caused his death. He believed in persuasion; I know not that he ever used harsh means, but would talk to me for hours together. As soon as it was dark he would call me to his side and begin to talk, and tell me that the Great Spirit would bless me with a long life if I should love my friends, and particularly the aged. He would always take me with him when going any where near, and I learned his movements, for I watched him going through the woods. Often would he tell me that when I should be a man that I must do so, and so, and do as he did, while fording the rivers, shooting the deer, trapping the beaver, etc., etc. I always imitated him while I was a hunter.

My mother was also kind and affectionate; she seemed to be happy when she saw us enjoying ourselves by her; often she would not eat much for days together; she would leave all for us! She was an industrious woman; in the spring she made more sugar than any one else; she was never idle while the season for gathering wild rice lasted.

I was taught early to hunt the deer. It was a part of our father's duty to teach us how to handle the gun as well as the bow and arrow. I was early reminded to hunt for myself; a thirst to excel in hunting began to increase; no pains were spared, no fatigue was too great, and at all seasons I found something to stimulate me to exertion, that I might become a good hunter. For years I followed my father, observed how he approached the deer, the manner of getting it upon his shoulders to carry it home. The appearance of the sky, the sound of distant water-falls in the morning, the appearance of the clouds and the winds, were to be noticed. The step, and the gesture, in traveling in search of the deer, were to be observed.

Many a lecture I received when the deer lay bleeding at the feet of my father; he would give me an account of the nobleness of the hunter's deeds, and said that I should never be in want whenever there was any game, and that many a poor aged man could be assisted by me. *"If you reverence the aged, many will be glad to hear of your name,"* were the words of my father. "The poor man will say to his children, 'my children, let us go to him, for he is a great hunter, and is kind to the poor, he will not turn us away empty.' The Great Spirit, who has given the aged a long life, will bless you. You must never laugh at any suffering object, for you know not how soon you may be in the same condition: never kill any game needlessly." Such was his language when we were alone in the woods. Ah! they were lessons directed from heaven.

In the spring but few deer were killed, because they were not in good order, the venison being poor, and the skin so thin, that it was no object to kill them. To hunt deer in the summer was my great delight, which I did in the following manner:—During the day I looked for their tracks, as they came on the shore of the lake or river during the night; they came there to feed. If they came on the bank of the river, I lighted pitch pine, and the current of the river took the canoe along the shore. My lantern was so constructed that the light could not fall on one spot, but swept along the shore. The deer could see the light, but were not alarmed by it, continued feeding on the weeds. In this way, I have approached so close that I could have reached them with my paddle. In this manner our forefathers shot them, not with a gun, as I did, but with the bow and arrow. Bows were made strong enough, so that the arrows might pierce through them.

Another mode of hunting on the lakes, preferred by some, is shooting without a light. Many were so expert, and possessed such an accuracy in hearing, that that they could shoot successfully in the dark, with no other guide than the noise of the deer in the water; the position of the deer being well known, in this way, the darkest night. I will here relate an occurrence which took place in 1834. My father and I were hunting on the river Trent, in the night; after we had shot two deer, and while returning homewards, we heard the noise of a deer's footsteps. The night was as dark as pitch. We approached the deer. I asked my father at what part of the animal I should aim. He replied, "at the head or neck." I poised my gun and fired; hearing no noise, I concluded that my game was sure. I lighted some pitch pine and walked towards the spot from which the noise had come. The deer lay dead and bleeding. On examination I found that I had shot it just below the ear. In the fall of the year, also, I was accustomed to hunt; the meat was very fine, and the skins, (from which our moccasons were made), were much thicker at this season. Those that could track the deer on fallen leaves and shoot one each day, were considered first rate hunters. The fall is the best time to determine the skill of the huntsman.

Of all animals the bear is the most dangerous to hunt. I had heard so many stories about its cunning that I dreaded to meet one. One day a party of us were going out to hunt the bear, just below Crooke's rapids. After we had made a temporary place to stay for several days, we marched in file; after a while we halted, each took a different direction. My father said, "my son you had better loiter behind the rest. Do not go far, for you may lose yourself." We parted—I took my course, and the rest theirs. I trembled for fear I should see what I was hunting for! I went only where I least expected to see a bear, and every noise I heard in the woods, I thought must be one. As I stood on an old mossy log, there was such a crack on the side of the hill that my heart leaped within me. As I turned and looked, there was a large bear running towards me! I hid myself behind a tree; but on he came; I watched him; he came like a hogshead rolling down hill; there were no signs of stopping; when a few feet from me, I jumped aside, and cried *Yah!* (an exclamation of fear). I fired my gun without taking sight; in turning suddenly to avoid me, he threw up the earth and leaves; for an instant I was led to believe that the bear was upon me. I dropped my gun and fell backwards, while the bear lay sprawling just by me. Having recovered, I took up my gun and went a few feet from where I fell, and loaded my gun in a hurry. I then sought for a long pole, and with it, I poked it on its side, to see if it was really dead. It did not move, it was dead; but even then I had not courage to go and touch it with my hands. When all was over, and I had told my father I had killed a bear, I felt as though my little leggings could hardly contain me. In examining it, I found the ball had gone through its heart.

Bear meat is like pork. It can be kept a long time when cured. For some weeks together this was the only kind of food we used to eat.

The oil of the bear is used for various purposes. One use is, to prevent the falling out of the hair. The apothecaries buy it from the Indians for about five dollars a gallon.

The skins of bears are what our forefathers wore, before the white people came amongst us, as blankets; but now *land-sharks,* called traders, buy them from the Indians for a mere trifle.

I loved to hunt the bear, the beaver, and the deer; but now, the occupation has no charms for me. I will now take the goose quill for my *bow,* and its point for my *arrow.* If perchance I may yet speak, when my poor aching head lies low in the grave; when the hand that wrote these recollections shall have crumbled into dust; then these pages will not have been written in vain.

> "O! Land of rest for thee I sigh—
> When will the season come,
> When I shall lay my armor by,
> And dwell in peace at home."

The beaver was hunted in the spring and fall. They were either trapped or shot. Among all the animals that live in the water, the beaver is of the kindest disposition, when tamed; it is a very cleanly animal; sits on its broad tail on the ground while feeding; feeds all night, and sleeps most of the day. The beaver skin was once worth from eight to ten dollars a piece, or four dollars per pound.

The otter, too, is much valued. The whites buy the skins, and make caps of them. They are mostly caught in traps. In the fall and spring they are always on the move.

The otter is a greedy animal; it can be tamed, but when hungry becomes cross, and often bites. If it be a half a mile off, it will scent any food preparing in the wigwam.

When about five years old, I commenced shooting birds, with a small bow and arrow. I have shot many a bird, but am no more a marksman. I used to feel proud when I use to carry home my own game. The first thing that any of the hunters shot, was cooked by the grandfather and grandmother, and there was great rejoicing, to inspire the youthful hunter with fresh ardor. Day after day I searched for the grey squirrel, the woodpecker, the snipe, and the snow bird, for this was all my employment.

The gun was another instrument put into my hands, which I was taught to use both carefully and skilfully. Seldom do accidents occur from the use of fire arms among our people. I delighted in running after the deer, in order to head and shoot them. It was a well known fact that I ranked high among the hunters. I remember the first deer I ever shot, it was about one mile north of the village of Keene. The Indians, as has just been said, once had a custom, which is now done away, of making a great feast of the first deer that a young hunter caught; the young hunter, however, was not to partake of any of it, but wait upon the others. All the satisfaction he could realize, was to thump his heels on the ground, while he and others were singing the following hunter's song:

"Ah yah ba wah, ne gah me koo nah vah!
Ah yah wa seeh, ne gah me koo nah nah."*

The fattest of the bucks I'll take,
The choicest of all animals I'll take.

In the days of our ignorance we used to dance around the fire. I shudder when I think of those days of our darkness. I thought the Spirit would be kind to me if I danced before the old men; and day after day, or night after night, I have been employed with others in this way. I thank God that those days will never return.

---

* These lines are sung over and over again, for about half an hour.

III

The Ojebwas, as well as many others, acknowledged that there was but one Great Spirit, who made the world; they gave him the name of good or benevolent; *kesha* is benevolent, *mone-doo* is spirit; Kesha-mon-e-doo. They supposed he lived in the heavens; but the most of the time he was in the *Sun*. They said it was from him they received all that was good through life, and that he seldom needs the offering of his Red children, for he was seldom angry.

They also said he could hear all his children, and see them. He was the author of all things that they saw, and made the other spirits that were acknowledged by the Ojebwas. It was said that these other spirits took special care of the various departments of nature. The god of the *hunter* was one who presided over the animals; the god of *war* was one who controlled the destinies of men; the god of *medicine* was one who presided over the herbs of the earth. The fishes had theirs, the birds had theirs, and there was another over the moon and stars!

> "Millions of spiritual creatures walk the earth
> Unseen, both when we sleep and when we wake."

There was one unappeasable spirit, called Bad Spirit, Mah-je-mah-ne-doo. He, it was thought, lived under the earth; and from him was attributed all that was not good, bad luck, sickness, even death. To him they offered sacrifices more than to any other spirit, things most dear to them. There were three things that were generally offered to the Bad Spirit, viz. a dog, whiskey, and tobacco, a fit offering with the exception of the poor dog. The poor dog was painted red on its paws, with a large stone and five plugs of tobacco tied about its neck; it was then sunk in the water; while the beating of the drum took place upon the shore, and words were chanted to the Bad Spirit.

The whiskey was thus offered to the Bad Spirit:—When the Indians were seated around the wigwam, or on the grass, and the person who deals out the whiskey had given all the Indians a dram then the devil was to have his share; it was poured on the ground, and if it went down quickly, it was thought he accepted the offering.

Fire water was sometimes poured out near the head of the graves of the deceased, that their spirits might drink with their former friends.

GEORGE COPWAY

I have often seen them sit around the grave, and as they drank, make mention of the name of their dead, and pour some whiskey on the ground.

Our religion consisted in observing certain ceremonies every spring. Most of the Ojebwas around us, use to come and worship the Great Spirit with us at Rice Lake. At this festival a great many of the youth were initiated into the medical mysteries of the nation. We were taught the virtues of herbs, and the various kinds of minerals used in our medicine. I will here describe the Me-tac-we-gah-mig or Grand Medicine Lodge. It was a wigwam 150 feet long and 15 feet wide. The clan of medicine men and women alone, were allowed to be inside, at each sitting, with their medicine badge, on each side of the wigwam. Then there were four old men who took the lead in singing, and beating the drum, as they stood near the centre. Before them were a company who were to take degrees. There were four grades in the institution; and as I have often thought, somewhat similar to the Masonic institution.

After the singing commenced, the whole company arose and danced, as they moved from one end of the wigwam to the other. As they go round, one-half of them cast their heads down upon their bosoms, as if affected by the medicine, which was kept in small skins, and which they pretended to thrust at each other; this was done to deceive the ignorant. These forms were continued several days. The party to be made medicine men and women, looked on in the mean time, to see what they would have to do themselves. Then they are taken to another place with our medicine men, and are taught the science of medicine. After receiving instructions, another day was allotted to give them instruction on morality. They were advised on various subjects. All were to keep silence, and endeavor to retain what they were taught. I will here give some of the sayings of our medicine men:—

"If you are a good hunter, warrior, and a medicine man, when you die, you will have no difficulty in getting to the far west in the spirit land."

"Listen to the words of your parents, never be impatient, then the Great Spirit will give you a long life."

"Never pass by any indigent person without giving him something to eat. Owh wah-yah-bak-mek ke-gah-shah-wa-ne-mig—the spirit that sees you will bless you."

"If you see an orphan in want, help him; for you will be rewarded by his friends here, or thanked by his parents in the land of spirits."

"If you own a good hunting dog, give it to the first poor man who really needs it."

"When you kill a deer, or bear, never appropriate it to yourself alone, if others are in want; never withhold from them what the Great Spirit has blessed you with."

"When you eat, share with the poor children who may be near you, for when you are old, they will administer to your wants."

"Never use improper medicine to the injury of another, lest you yourself may receive the same treatment."

"When an opportunity offers, call the aged together, and provide for them venison properly cooked, and give them a hearty welcome; then the gods that have favored them will be your friends."

These are a few specimens of the advice given by our fathers, and by adhering to their counsels, the lives, peace, and happiness, of the Indian race were secured; for then there was no whiskey amongst them. O! that accursed thing. O! why did the white man give it to my poor fathers? None but fiends in human shape could have introduced it amongst us.

I recollect the day when my people in Canada were both numerous and happy; and since then, to my sorrow, they have faded away like frost before the heat of the sun! Where are now that once numerous and happy people? The voice of but few is heard.

The Ojebwa nation, that unconquered nation, has fallen a prey to the withering influence of intemperance. Their buoyant spirits could once mount the air as on the wings of a bird. Now they have no spirits. They are hedged in, bound, and maltreated, by both the American and the British Governments. They have no other hope, than that at some day, they will be relieved from their privations and trials by death. The fire-water has rolled towards them like the waves of the sea. Alas! alas! my poor people! The tribe became dissipated, and consequently improvident, and often suffered intensely. It was in visiting the interior that we always suffered most.

I will here narrate a single circumstance which will convey a correct idea of the sufferings to which Indians were often exposed. To collect furs of different kinds, for the traders, we had to travel far into the woods, and remain there the whole winter. Once we left Rice Lake in the fall, and ascended the river in canoes, above Bellmont Lake. There were five families about to hunt with my father, on his grounds. The winter began to set in, and the river having frozen over, we left the canoes, the dried venison, the beaver, and some flour and pork; and when we had gone farther north, say about sixty miles from the whites, for the purpose of hunting, the snow fell for five days in succession to such a depth, that it was impossible to shoot or trap any thing. Our provisions were exhausted, and we had no means to procure any more. Here we were. The snow about five feet deep; our wigwam buried; the branches of the trees falling around us, and cracking from the weight of the snow.

Our mother boiled birch bark for my sister and myself, that we might not starve. On the seventh day some of them were so weak that they could not raise themselves, and others could not stand alone. They could only crawl in and out of the wigwam. We parched beaver skins and old moccasons for food. On the ninth day none of the men were able to go abroad, except my father and uncle. On the tenth day, still being without food, those only who were able to walk about the wigwam, were my father, my grand-mother, my sister, and myself. O how distressing to see the starving Indians lying about the wigwam with hungry and eager looks; the children would cry for something to eat. My poor mother would heave *bitter sighs of despair*, the tears falling from her cheeks profusely as she kissed us. Wood, though plenty, could not be obtained, on account of the feebleness of our limbs.

My father, at times, would draw near the fire, and rehearse some prayer to the gods. It appeared to him that there was no way of escape; the men, women and children dying; some of them were speechless. The wigwam was cold and dark, and covered with snow. On the eleventh day, just before daylight, my father fell into a sleep; he soon awoke and said to me, "My son, the Great Spirit is about to bless us; this night in my dream I saw a person coming from the east, walking on the tops of the trees. He told me that we should obtain two beavers this morning about nine o'clock. Put on your moccasons and go along with me to the river, and we will hunt the beaver, perhaps for the last time." I saw that his countenance beamed with delight; he was full of confidence. I put on my moccasons and carried my snow shoes, staggering along behind him, about half a mile. Having made a fire near the river, where there was an air hole, through which the beaver had come up during the night, my father tied a gun to a stump, with the muzzle towards the air hole; he also tied a string to the trigger, and said "should you see the beaver rise, pull the string and you will kill it." I stood by the fire with the string in my hand. I soon heard a noise occasioned by the blow of his tomahawk; he had killed a beaver, and he brought it to me. As he laid it down, he said "then the Great Spirit will not let us die here;" adding, as before, "if you see the beaver, rise, and pull the string." He left me, I soon saw the nose of one; but I did not shoot. Presently another came up; I pulled the trigger, and off the gun went. I could not see for sometime for the smoke. My father ran towards me, took the two beavers and laid them side by side; then pointing to the sun, said, "Do you see the sun? The Great Spirit informed me that we should kill these two about this time this morning. We will yet see our relatives at Rice Lake; now let us go home and see if they are still alive." We hastened home, and arrived just in time to save them from death. Since which, we visited the same spot, the year after the missionaries came among us. My father, with feelings of gratitude, knelt down on the spot where we had nearly perished. Glory to God! But what have I done for Him since? Comparatively nothing. We were just at death's door, when Christianity rescued us. I have heard of many, who have perished in this way, far in the woods. In my travels to the west, I have met many whose families had perished, and who had themselves merely escaped starvation. May God forgive me, for my ingratitude and indolence in his blessed cause!

I will here introduce a favorite war song of the Ojebwa nation. It was accompanied by dancing, and an occasional war-whoop. At the end of each stanza, a warrior rehearsed some former victories, which inspired them with ardor for war. Unchristianized Indians are often like greedy lions after their prey; yes, at times, they are indeed cruel and blood thirsty. I have met with warriors, who, when they had killed their enemies, cut open their breasts, took out their hearts, and drank their blood; and all this was out of mere *revenge*. But to the *War Song*, which was first translated for Col. McKinney, *"the Indian's friend,"* on the shore of Lake Superior.

> "On that day when our heroes lay low—lay low—
> On that day when our heroes lay low,
> I fought by their side, and thought ere I died,
> Just vengeance to take on the foe—the foe—
> Just vengeance to take on the foe.
>
> "On that day when our chieftains lay dead—lay dead—
> On that day when our chieftains lay dead,

I fought hand to hand, at the head of my band,
And here, on my breast, have I bled—have I bled—
And here, on my breast, have I bled.

"Our chiefs shall return no more—no more—
Our chiefs shall return no more—
And their brothers in war who can't show scar for scar,
Like women their fates shall deplore—shall deplore—
Like women, their fates shall deplore.

"Five winters in hunting we'll spend—we'll spend—
Five winters in hunting we'll spend—
Then our youths grown to men, to the war lead again,
And our days like our fathers', we'll end—we'll end—
And our days like our fathers', we'll end."

IV

Our people believed much in omens. The barking of foxes and of wolves, the bleating of the deer, the screeching of owls, bad luck in hunting, the flight of uncommon kinds of birds, the moaning noise of a partridge, the noise of a *chuck chuck ske sey*,* were ominous of ill; the two last were certain omens of death. But the sailing of an eagle to and fro, and the noise of a raven, were omens of good.

Dreams, too, were much relied on by our nation. They thought the spirits revealed to them what they were to do, and what they should be, viz. good hunters, warriors, and medicine men. I would fast sometimes two, and sometimes even four days. When fasting, we were to leave the wigwam early in the morning, and travel all day from one place to another, in search of the favor of the gods. I was taught to believe that the gods would communicate with me, in the shape of birds, animals, etc., etc. When I fell asleep in the woods, and dreamed some strange dream, I felt confident that it was from the spirits. I will now relate what I dreamed when I was but twelve years old, and also my father's interpretation of my dream.

Myself and others were sleeping far from the wigwam, near a large pine. I saw, in my dream, a person coming from the east; he approached, walking on the air; he looked down upon me, and said, "Is this where you are?" I said "yes." "Do you see this pine?" "Yes, I see it." "It is a great and high tree." I observed that the tree was lofty, reaching towards the heavens. Its branches extended over land and water, and its roots were very deep. "Look on it while I sing, yes, gaze upon the tree." He sang, and pointed to the tree; it commenced waving its top; the earth about its roots was heaved up, and the waters roared and tossed from one side of their beds to the other. As soon as he stopped singing, and let fall his hands, every thing became perfectly still and quiet. "Now," said he, "sing the words which I have sung." I commenced as follows:—

---

* To this bird I have given its *Indian* name, because I have not been able to discover it among the collection of the various birds in the books and in the museums. It is about the size of the smaller kind of parrot. The color of its feathers is like those of a jay, having short wings small and broad peak, with an upper and lower row of teeth, like a human being. In this last respect, it is different from any other bird. It takes its name from the sounds it utters, viz. *chuck, chuck*. I hope that the celebrated ornithologist Audabon, to whom I intend to present a copy of my work, will throw some light upon this subject.

"It is I who travel in the winds,
It is I who whisper in the breeze,
I shake the trees,
I shake the earth,
I trouble the waters on every land."

While singing, I heard the winds whistle, saw the tree waving its top, the earth heaving, heard the waters roaring, because they were all troubled and agitated. Then said he, "I am from the rising of the sun, I will come and see you again. You will not see me often; but you will hear me speak." Thus spoke the spirit, and then turned away towards the road from which he had come. I told my father of my dream, and after hearing all, he said, "My son, *the god of the winds* is kind to you; the aged tree, I hope, may indicate long life; the wind may indicate that you will travel much; the water which you saw, and the winds, will carry your canoe safely through the waves."

I relied much on my dream, for then I knew no better. But, however little reliance can be placed in dreams, yet may not the Great Spirit take this method, sometimes, to bring about some good result?

There was no such thing known among our people as swearing, or profaning the name of the Great Spirit in vain. The whites first taught them to swear. I often swore, when I knew not what I said. I have seen some *white faces*, with *black hearts*, who took delight in teaching them to profane the name of God. O merciless, heartless, and wicked white men, may a merciful God forgive you your enormous turpitude and recklessness!

There was a custom among us, before christianity visited us, that when the Ojebwas intended to take a general whiskey "spree," several young men were appointed by the head chief to collect all the fire arms, knives, war-clubs and other weapons, and keep them in a secret place, till the Indians had completed their frolic. This was done to prevent them from murdering each other when intoxicated. By this means many lives have been saved; although many have been killed during their drunken fights. They would walk very far, for a dram of liquor. I once heard of an individual, whom I had seen many times, who would travel all day for a single drink of fire-water. When he arrived at the trading post, he obtained and guzzled down a cup full of whiskey. When the poison had operated, he said, that he felt as if his head was going down his throat; and added, "Whah! I wish my neck was a mile long, so that I might feel and hear the whiskey running all the way down!"

A certain Indian once teased a Mrs. F. for whiskey, which he said was to cure his "*big toe,*" that had been badly bruised the preceding night. Mrs. F. said, "I am afraid you will drink it." He declared he would not drink it; and after much pleading, she handed him some; he took it, and looking first at his toe, and then at the liquor, alternately, all of a sudden he slipped the whiskey down his gullet, at the same time exclaiming, as he pointed to his toe, "There, *whiskey,* go down to my poor big toe."

One of our people, who had much resolution, and was determined to seek religion, when he heard that the Methodist Indians were not to drink any more fire-water, remarked as follows:—

"*Well, if that is the case, I'll go tonight, and bid my old friend whiskey a final farewell.*" He went, and drank and caroused with his rum-companions all night. On the following day about noon, he came staggering towards his wigwam, singing out to all whom he met, "*Me goes to Methodist, me no drink little more, me am Methodist.*" He was true to his word, for he drank no more, and the Lord blessed him in the forgiveness of all his sins. For eighteen years he was a consistent Christian, and died last June, with the brightest hopes of immortal bliss. Oh! the heights and depths of the goodness and mercy of God!

In view of these things, I have often exclaimed from the bottom of my heart, in the language of "The Indian's Regret," and which is the language of all, who have been brought from darkness, to the marvelous light of the gospel:—

> "*O had our Indian fathers known*
> *What Prophets told of Christ and heaven!*
> *For them, we drop a tear and mourn,*
> *But weep for joy, our sins forgiven.*"

V

The *traditions* handed down from father to son, were held very sacred; one half of these are not known by the white people, however far their researches may have extended. There is an unwillingness, on the part of the Indians to communicate many of their traditions. The only way to come at these is, to educate the Indians, so that they may be able to write out what they have heard, or may hear, and publish it. Should I be spared till next summer, I design to visit my people in the far west, and abide with them long enough to learn the rest of their traditions, with an account of their migration to this country. My own belief is, that they came to this country, and fought with the original inhabitants; and having overpowered them, became the owners of the soil. I will not now give my reasons for this belief, as I expect at some future day to collect all the necessary information for this purpose, from history and discoveries, corroborated by these traditions. My readers will then be able to judge whether we are to be identified with the dispersed and "lost tribes of Israel." Can it be possible, that, had we sprung from any of the Hebrew tribes, we should be so completely ignorant of a Messiah, a Sabbath, or a single vestige of the Levitical Law? But enough of this for the present.

As far as I am able to learn, our nation has never been conquered; and have maintained their ground wherever they have conquered. The *Saxe* tribe have tried their ingenuity, power, and bravery, to drive them from the south shore of Lake Superior. The *Hurons* mustered their warriors against the aggressions made by the Ojebwa nation. Their war-canoes, were once directed against the Ojebwa nation, but they were obliged to turn back, and flee for protection, to the Shawnee nation. The sound of the war-whoop which once rang all around the shores of Lake Huron, receded, and died away on the waters of Sandusky. The arms that once wielded the war-club, were strewed about their grounds, on account of broken treaties made in former days, and massacres at the mouth of French river. The *Iraquois*, who struck terror wherever their mere names were mentioned, also tried to check our progress, after we had conquered the Hurons. Their war-whoops resounded over the dismal regions of the conquered land; but they too shared the same fate. They went as spies as far as La Pointe, on the south shore of Lake Superior; but not with their armies any farther than Ke-wa-o-non, in the copper regions. Here they were massacred by hundreds, and fell in their canoes at one of the narrow passes, on their way to the Portage, about fourteen miles from the Bay of Aunce. After these fruitless attempts to drive the Ojebwas from their land, they fought many battles with them in the regions now called Canada West; but in these they suffered much, and were defeated. It was then, probably, that the Hurons and Iraquois leagued together, hoping by their combined forces to conquer us. This accounts for the confederacy that existed when the whites came among them.

The migration of the Ojebwas has been traced from the upper part of Lake Superior, and even several hundred miles above its head, along the shore of Lake Superior, down to Lake Huron, St. Clair, the foot of Lake Michigan, north of Lakes Erie and Ontario, and some distance down the St. Lawrence.

They now inhabit a portion of land extending about two thousand miles east and west, and from two hundred and fifty to three hundred miles from north to south. They have in each village, a chief who governs them, besides a great number of war chiefs. Each village has a council of its own, made up of the different tribes. A tribe is a band of Indians whose sign or mark is the same; for example, such as wear the sign of the *crane*, recognize each other as relatives; and although each village may be composed of different tribes, yet they must be of the same nation.

Councils of peace must be held by two nations. These councils are held in high esteem. When two nations are at war, if either sues for peace, they hand to each other some token, such as a belt of wampum (or beads), or a calumet (a long pipe).

There was once a general council held, between the Hurons and the Ojebwas; it was conducted in the following manner:—They came together near Sault St. Marie, and agreed upon a peace for five years. After the pipe of peace was prepared, the Ojebwa and the Huron warriors arranged themselves in two lines, on each side of their chiefs, and said that they must ascertain whether the Great Spirit would approve of their proceedings. Two from each nation were chosen; the Hurons held the pipe filled with tobacco, the Ojebwas, the steel, flint, and spunk. The steel was then struck against the flint, and if, on the first stroke, the spunk was ignited, so as to fire the tobacco, and thus enable the warrior to draw in, and to emit, a volume of smoke, then the evidence was complete that the Great Spirit approved of their plans and proceedings; and the whole assembly now would set up the most tremendous shout of joy. The two nations were successful in this. The shout was given, peace was secured, and these two powerful nations separated for their own homes. For three years no dark cloud hung over the two nations.

The Ojebwas began to trade with the whites at Quebec. It usually required all the summer to journey from the shore of Lake Superior to that place and back again. These were tedious and perilous journeys; but they were determined to obtain "*the snake which spit fire, smoke, and death*"; this was their description of *a gun* to their brethren.

It was during these journeys that forty of them were massacred by the Hurons, at the mouth of French River, without the least provocation; plunder alone was their object. This, in connection with similar acts, occasioned that war which resulted in their complete extermination from Canada by our nation.

The *future state* of the Ojebwas, was in the *Far West*. They described that state or country, *as being full of game*, and with *trees loaded with fruit of every description.*

When an Indian warrior died on the field of battle, his soul, it was said, took its immediate flight to this paradise. The souls of those, however, who died in other circumstances, it was believed, departed from the grave, and journeyed in the ordinary way, although unseen by mortals, to this same land.

There was a difficult bridge near this land, over which the soul was to cross. A warrior, hunter, or medicine man, would have no difficulty in crossing this bridge. Under this bridge was a rapid stream, and he who was not a good warrior, hunter or medicine man, would either fall into the water, or lose his way, after having crossed, in some barren country, where there was no game, or fruit, although there might be, occasionally, a deer, or the like. O how barren! How dismal! A place where distress, want, and despair would continue! On the other hand, the favored warrior entered the fields of paradise, amidst the shouts and welcome of his fellow warriors, who had preceded him to this land of plenty. The deer, the moose, the elk, and all kinds of animals, fruits, flowers, and the singing of birds fill and charm the land. While the ever rolling valleys are visited with delightful and refreshing winds. To kill, eat, and shoot, are their only employments. No sickness, no fatigue, no death, will ever visit them. The valleys and the mountains are to be clothed with evergreens. No winter to chill the earth. A carnal heaven indeed! A sensual paradise! Oh! the credulous and misguided Indian.

"Lo! the poor Indian whose untutored mind,
Sees God in clouds, or hears him in the wind;
Whose soul's proud science never taught to stray,
Beyond the solar walk or milky way.
Yet simple nature his hopes has given
Beyond the cloud top'd hill a humble heaven,
Some safer world in depths of woods embrace,
Some Island in the watery waste.
Where slaves once more their native land behold,
No fiends torment, nor Christian thirsts for gold."

—Pope

My father often spoke of that country, while I was young. He informed me, that if I should become a great warrior, a hunter, or a medicine man, I would have no difficulty in reaching that happy spot. Little then did he know of a *heaven revealed in the gospel*. That heaven, where angels and pure spirits dwell, and where we shall see the blessed Jesus as he is, and, what is still a greater honor, be like him.

"O for a thousand tongues to sing
My great Redeemer's praise!
The glories of my God and King,
The triumphs of his grace!

"My gracious Master, and my God,
Assist me to proclaim,
To spread through all the earth abroad
The honors of thy Name.

"Jesus! the Name that charms our fears,
That bids our sorrows cease;
'Tis music in the sinner's ears,
'Tis life, and health, and peace."

"Oh uh pa-gish ke che ingo' dwok,
Neej uh ne she nah baig,
Che nuh nuh guh mo tuh wah wod
Ning e zha Mun e-doom.

"Ning e che Noo sa weej e shin,
Che ween duh mah ga yon,
O mah a ne gook kuh me gog
A zhe wa be ze yun.

"Jesus! kah be 'non duh we 'nung,
Kah gah see beeng wa 'nung;
Ka gait 'che me no ne kah zo,
Kah noo je mo e nung."

When our warriors were dying, they told their children that they would soon reach the happy country. Their eyeballs, rolling in death, were turned towards the setting Sun. O white man! why did you not tell us before, that there was a better heaven than that of the Indian's? Did not the blessed Saviour command, "Go ye into *all* the world, and preach the gospel to every creature?" Reader, almost by the door of your churches, my forefathers perished for the lack of the bread of life, while you have reached out your arms, and extended your means for the relief of those *in distant lands!* O what a thought! Thousands have already perished, and thousands more will yet perish, unless converted to God! The thought of *perishing!* how *insufferable!* O, how *intolerable!*

> "O mercy, O mercy, look down from above;
> Great Creator, on us, thy sad children, with love;
> When beneath to their darkness the wicked are driven,
> May our justified souls find a welcome in heaven."

VI

Rice Lake, that beautiful lake, extends about twenty-five miles, and is from two to three miles in breadth, running from northeast to southwest. It contains about twenty islands. Large quantities of wild rice abound in almost every part of the lake; it resembles fields of wheat. As ducks of all kinds resort here in great abundance, to feed upon the rice, consequently, there is much good game in the fall of the year. They fly in large flocks, and often appear like clouds. Some of the islands just referred to, are beautiful; for example, *Sugar Island*, with its beautiful edge of evergreens near the water; *Spoke Island*, a place of fashionable summer resort. One of the largest of these islands, contains about three hundred acres.

In 1818, our people surrendered to the British government a large part of their territory, for the sum of £750; reserving, as they had good reason to believe, all the islands. As they could neither read nor write, they were ignorant of the fact that these islands were *included* in the sale. They were repeatedly told by those who purchased for the government, that the islands were *not* included in the articles of agreement. But since that time, some of us have learned to read, and to our utter astonishment, and to the everlasting disgrace of that *pseudo* christian nation, we find that we have been most grossly abused, deceived, and cheated. Appeals have been frequently made, but all in vain.

Rice Lake contains quantities of the finest fish. In the summer, great numbers of boats may be seen trowling for *mascalounge*, a species of pike, some of which weigh about thirty pounds. Bass, eels, etc., are also found in this lake. Since locks have been made on the canal down to Crooke's rapids, much fur can be procured all around the lake, especially *muskrats*—Shah-won-dase O dah me koo mun.

This is the spot on which I roamed during my early days. Often have I gone with my birch-bark canoe from island to island, in quest of ducks and fish. The plain on the south shore, is called Whortleberry Plain. A steamboat runs from Gore's Landing to Peterboro once a day.

The village of the Ojebwas is on the north; the land gradually slopes towards the water. Its farms, church, school house, and council house, can be seen at a considerable distance. It was here where the Rev. James Evans, whose obituary was noticed in the following manner in the

"Albany Evening Journal," December 22, 1846, first taught an Indian school.

"Suddenly, on the 23rd of November, at Keelby, England, Rev. JAMES EVANS, for many years a Wesleyan missionary in Canada, and the territory of the Hudson Bay Company. On Sunday, the 22nd, he preached twice, and on Monday evening 23rd, spoke at a missionary meeting, with great fervency. He had complained of a slight indisposition, previous to the meeting, but after he had finished his address, he said that "his indisposition had been completely removed." Soon after his head fell back, and life was gone."

He was a missionary in every sense of the word. From Rice Lake, he went to Lake Superior, and afterwards to the Hudson Bay Territory, where he labored with much success. His precious life was spent in rescuing the Ojebwa nation from misery and degradation. Fatigue, and hunger, were often his companions; but the power of living faith was that on which his soul feasted. O thou man of God, enviable are thy labors, thy rest, and thy glory! I, myself, still hold in sweet remembrance the sacred truths which thou didst teach me, even the commands of the MOST HIGH! *Memory*, like an angel, will still hover over the sacred spot, where first you taught me the letters of the Alphabet.

There are numerous lakes near Rice Lake; about some of which, the Ojebwas reside; particularly Mud, Schoogaug and Balsam Lakes. The country, in this vicinity, is rapidly increasing in population; the whites are continually settling among us. The deer was plenty a few years ago, but now only a few can be found. The Ojebwas are, at present, employed in farming instead of hunting; many of them have good and well cultivated farms. They not only raise grain enough for their own use, but often sell much to the whites.

The Canadian Commissioners on Indian affairs, in their report to Parliament in 1845, remarked, in relation to the Rice Lake Indians, as follows:—"These Indians are Methodists, and have either a resident missionary, or have been regularly visited by the missionary belonging to the Alnwick settlement. They have a school, and a schoolmaster is supported by the Methodist Missionary Society."

VII

The missionaries first visited us, on the island called *Be-quah-qua-yong*, in 1827, under the following circumstances. My father and I went to Port Hope, to see our principal trader, John D. Smith, in order to obtain goods and whiskey, about twelve miles from Rice Lake. After my father had obtained the goods, he asked for whiskey. Mr. Smith said, "John, do you know that whiskey will yet kill you, if you do not stop drinking? Why, all the Indians at Credit River, and at Grape Island, have abandoned drinking, and are now Methodists. I cannot give you any whiskey."

"*Tah yah!* (an exclamation of surprise), *it cannot be, I must* have whiskey to carry home; my people expect it," said my father. He wished to buy a barrel, but only obtained, after much pleading, about five gallons. My father *promised* to drink no more when the missionaries shall have come to Rice Lake. We reached home the same day about one o'clock, and the Indians were awaiting our arrival, that they might have some fire-water. They assembled themselves together and began to drink and to smoke. Many of them were sitting on the grass when the whiskey began to steal away their brains. One of our number suddenly ran in the crowd, and said, "*the black coats* (missionaries) are coming, and are on the other side of the point." Each looked at the other with perfect astonishment. My father said to our informer, "invite them to come over to us;" and to the one who was dealing out whiskey, "cover the keg with your blanket, and don't let the black coats see it." The whiskey was concealed, and then came the messengers of glad tidings of great joy. They were converted Indians, saved by grace, and had been sent to preach to us, and to invite us to attend a camp meeting near Cobourg. After shaking hands all around, one of them delivered a speech to the half drunken Indians. He referred to the day, when they were without the good news of *salvation*. He spoke with great earnestness, and the tears fell from his eyes. He said, "*Jesus Christ, Ke-sha-mon-e-doo O-gwe-son* (i.e. the Benevolent Spirit's son), came down to the world, and died to save the people; all the Indians at the Credit River, and Grape Island, are now on their road to the place where the Saviour has gone. Jesus has left a book containing his commands and sayings to all the world; you *will see it, and hear it read,* when you go to Cobourg, for the black coats have it. They wish you to come and hear it. Tomorrow is the *Sabbath,* and on that day we do not hunt, or work, for it is the day which the Great Spirit made for himself." He described the way that the Son of God was crucified. I observed some of them crying; my mother heaved deep sighs; the half drunken Indians were struck dumb, and hung their heads. Not a word was uttered. The missionaries said, "We will *sing*, and then we will *kneel down*, and *pray* to the Great Spirit." He gave out the following hymn:—

> "Jesus ish pe ming kah e zhod."
> "Jesus, my all, to heaven is gone."

They stood up and sang. O what sweet melody was in their voices! The echo was so great that there appeared to be a great many more singers than we could see. After the hymn, they prayed with the same fervency as they sung.

Peter Wason prayed, and in his prayer said, "O Great Spirit! here are some of my own relatives; open their eyes and save them!" After the prayer, they said they were going to Cobourg that evening; and if any desired to go with them, they would be glad to have them do so.

My father arose, and took the keg of whiskey, stepped into one of the small canoes, and paddled some thirty feet from the shore; here he poured out the whiskey into the lake, and threw the keg away. He then returned and addressed us in the following manner:—"You have all heard what our Brother said to us; I am going with them this evening; if any of you will go, do so this evening; the children can attend the great meeting some other time." Every one ran at once, to the paddles and canoes; and in a few minutes we were on the water. The missionaries had a skiff, in which they went from the Island to the opposite side. They sang again, and their very oars seemed to keep time on the still water. O how charming! The scenery of the water; the canoes moving in files, crossing the lake to visit their first camp meeting. When we arrived on the other side, it was about dusk, and we bought five candles for a *dollar* (!), and obtained an old lantern. We marched on a new road, the whole of Saturday night, in order to reach the camp ground. During the journey, we had to wade through deep creeks. Just before the dawn, we were about half a mile from the camp ground; here we tarried until day light, and then approached the camp.

When the Indians beheld the fence and the gate, and a great number of whites, they began to feel rather timid and suspicious, for the trader had told my father at Rice Lake, that *it was for the purpose of killing all the Indians* that the black coats had invited them to the meeting. My father told me to keep away from the ground, and hunt birds and squirrels with my bow and arrow; his object was to save my life, in the event of the Indians being killed. After remaining on the camp ground awhile, I departed; but while there, I saw a large number of converted Indians who belonged to Credit River, and Grape Island. Some of them were singing, some praying, and others lying about the ground as if dead. There were a great many preachers present.

On the third day many of our company were converted; among this number was my dear father!

As I entered the ground in the afternoon, I heard many voices, and among them my father's voice. I thought my father was dying; I ran to him, and found him lying partly on one of the seats. My father, said I, what is the matter with you? Are you sick? "Come here my son, I am not sick, but I am happy in my heart;" he placed his hand upon his breast while he spoke. "I told you that you must keep away from the ground, that your life might be spared; but I find that these are good, and not bad, people; kneel down and I will pray for you." I knelt, while he prayed. O, this was *my father's first prayer!* Me thinks, that at this time the angels rejoiced in heaven. I became agitated; my bow and arrows had fallen from my hand. The Indians lay about me like dead men. All this was the effect of the power of gospel grace, that had spread among them. The shouts, praises, and prayers, of fathers, mothers, sons, and daughters, were heard from every quarter. Those who had just appeared as dead, arose, and shouted the praises of God! They clapped their hands, and exclaimed, *"Jesus nin ge shah wa ne mig,"* Jesus has blessed me. The feeling was so general and powerful, that the influence was felt throughout the camp, both by the Indians and the whites. This was one of the happiest seasons I ever witnessed, except the season of my own conversion. Many of my relatives were converted on this occasion. Many of them have since gone to the world of spirits, and are now singing the praises of redeeming love. This *heavenly fire* began to spread from the camp, to Mud, Schoogaug and Balsam Lakes, the homes of the Ojebwas; also to the shores of Lake Simeco, and Lake Huron, and to the vicinity of Lake Superior.

"Waft, waft, ye winds his story,
And you ye waters roll,

Till like a sea of glory
It spreads from pole to pole."

On the camp ground, the Ojebwas sat in squads, giving and receiving instruction in singing, learning and teaching the Lord's prayer, and other things. Some were singing,

"Jesus, kuh ba ke zhig
Ning ee e nuh uh moz,
Uh pa gish kuh ke nuh wahb' dum 'wod
Ning ee 'nuh da moosh
A zhe o ne zhe shing,
O ge che o duh nuh me ah win."

"Jesus all the day long
Was my joy and my song;
O that all, his salvation might see!
He hath lov'd me, I cried;
He hath suffer'd and died
To redeem such a rebel as me."

VIII

The *conversion of my mother* took place during the summer, on Poutash Island, where the Indians had erected a bark chapel. For two years she lived in the enjoyment of religion. Before this chapel was ready she would call us together in the wigwam, and pray with and for us, several times a day, whether our father was at home or not. I remember well, at this moment, the language of her prayers.

She was taken sick in the winter of 1829, and was confined to her bed, most of the time, for three months; her disease was consumption. During these three months, she enjoyed much religion; there was not a day, in which she did not speak of Jesus and his promises with the greatest confidence and delight.

When she grew worse, she called for the class leaders to pray with her. She said to her mother, whom she supposed would die first, because her hair was *white*, "you will still live, but I am going to die, and will see Jesus first; soon, however, you will follow me."

The spirit of my dear mother took its flight on the 27th day of February, 1830. Just before her death, she prayed with her children; and advised us to be good Christians, to love Jesus, and to meet her in heaven. She then sang her favorite hymn,

> *"Jesus ish pe ming kah e zhod."*
> *"Jesus, my all, to heaven is gone."*

This was the first hymn she had ever heard or learned; and it is on this account that I introduce and sing this sweet hymn whenever I lecture "On the origin, history, traditions, migration, and customs, of the Ojebwa nation." We all knelt again by her bed side, and while clapping her hands, and endeavoring to shout for joy, she swooned away in death. The last words, which she feebly uttered, were, *"Jesus, Jesus."* Her spirit then fled, her lips were cold, and those warm hands that had so often and so faithfully administered comfort and relief, were now stiff. I looked around the wigwam; my father, sister, and brother sat near me, wringing their hands; they were filled with bitter grief, and appeared inconsolable, I then began to understand and appreciate fully her kindness and love. Who, who can, or will, take the place of a *mother*? Who will pray for us when we are sick or in distress? Her body was consigned to the grave without any parade. No church bell was tolled; but the whistling wind sounded through the woods. I have often knelt down, at the head of her grave, and wished that the time would soon arrive when it might please God to relieve me from my troubles and cares, and conduct me to the abode of my beloved parent. My sister Sarah too, who has since died, is doubtless with my mother. O how glorious the thought, *that both are now in heaven!* There is one spot where none will sigh for home. The flowers that blossom there, will never fade; the crystal waters that wind along those verdant vales, will never cease to send up their heavenly music; the clusters hanging from the trees overshadowing its banks, will be immortal clusters; and the friends that meet, will meet forever.

Little then did I think that I should have to pass through so many afflictions, and so many hardships. O my mother, I am still in a *cold, uncharitable, miserable world!* But the thought that thou art happy and blessed, is truly sweet and encouraging! It is this fact, and my own hopes of future bliss, that buoys me up, and sustains me in the hours of conflict and despondency. Although many years have elapsed, since her death, still, I often weep with mingled joy and grief when I think of my dear mother. "Blessed are the dead who die in the Lord." "I am not ashamed of the gospel of Christ, for it is the power of God unto salvation to every one that believeth." The gospel is the only remedy for the miseries and sins of the world.

My mother and sister's cases are not the only ones that I could relate concerning the happy lives and deaths of those once degraded and benighted Indians. Many have already reached heaven; and many more are now rejoicing on their road thither. Who will now say that the poor Indians cannot be converted? The least that Christians could have done, was to send the gospel among them, after having dispossessed them of their lands; thus preparing them for usefulness here, and happiness hereafter. Let no one say that I am ungrateful in speaking thus. It was the *duty* of Christians to send us missionaries; and it is *now* their duty to send *more* of them. There are still 25,000 of my poor brethren in darkness, and without the gospel. Let the prayers of all the churches ascend to the Most High, in their behalf, that He who has power to deliver, may save the poor Indian from misery, ignorance, and perdition.

IX

In the summer following my mother's death (1830), *I was converted*. The following are the circumstances connected with my conversion. My father and I attended a camp meeting near the town of Colbourne. On our way from Rice Lake, to the meeting, my father held me by the hand, as I accompanied him through the woods. Several times he prayed with me, and encouraged me to seek religion at this camp meeting. We had to walk thirty miles under a hot sun, in order to reach the place of destination. Multitudes of Indians, and a large concourse of whites from various places, were on the ground when we arrived. In the evening, one of the white preachers (Wright, I believe was his name), spoke; his text was, "For the great day of His wrath is come, and who shall be able to stand." He spoke in English, and as he closed each sentence, an Indian preacher gave its interpretation. He spoke of the plain and good road to heaven; of the characters that were walking in it; he then spoke of the bad place, the judgment, and the coming of a Saviour. I now began to feel as if I should die, *I felt very sick in my heart*. Never had I felt so before; I was deeply distressed, and knew not the cause. I resolved to go and prostrate myself at the mourners bench, as soon as an opportunity offered. We were now invited to approach. I went to the bench and knelt down by the roots of a large tree. But how could I pray? I did not understand how to pray; and besides, I thought that the Great Spirit was *too great* to listen to the words of a poor Indian boy. What added to my misery was, that it had rained in torrents about three quarters of an hour, and I was soaking wet. The thunder was appalling, and the lightning terrific. I then tried again to pray, but I was not able. I did not know what words to use. My father then prayed with and for me. Many were praising God, all around me. The storm now ceased, and nearly all the lights had been extinguished by the rain. I still groaned and agonized over my sins. I was so agitated and alarmed that I knew not which way to turn in order to get relief. I was like a *wounded bird*, fluttering for its life. Presently and suddenly, I saw in my mind, something approaching; it was like a small but brilliant torch; it appeared to pass through the leaves of the trees. My poor body became so enfeebled that I fell; my heart trembled. The small brilliant light came near to me, and fell

GEORGE COPWAY

upon my head, and then ran all over and through me, just as if water had been copiously poured out upon me. I knew not how long I had lain after my fall; but when I recovered, my head was in a puddle of water, in a small ditch. I arose; and O! how happy I was! I felt as light as a feather. I clapped my hands, and exclaimed in English, "*Glory to Jesus.*" I looked around for my father, and saw him. I told him that I had found "Jesus." He embraced me, and kissed me; I threw myself into his arms. I felt as strong as a lion, yet as humble as a poor Indian boy saved by grace, by grace alone. During that night I did not sleep. The next morning, my cousin, George Shawney, and myself, went out into the woods to sing and pray. As I looked at the trees, the hills, and the vallies, O how beautiful they all appeared! I looked upon them, as it were, with new eyes and new thoughts. Amidst the smiles of creation, the birds sang sweetly, as they flew from tree to tree. We sang

"Jesus the name that charms our fears."

O how sweet the recollections of that day! "Jesus all the day long was my joy and my song." Several hundred were converted during this meeting. Many of the Indians were reluctant to leave the camp ground when the meeting was broken up. When we reached our homes at Rice Lake, every thing seemed to me as if it wore a different aspect; every thing was clothed with beauty. Before this, I had only begun to spell and read. I now resumed my studies with a new and different relish. Often, when alone, I prayed that God would help me to qualify myself to teach others how to read the word of God; this circumstance I had not told to any one. On Sabbath mornings I read a chapter in the New Testament, which had been translated for my father before we went to meeting.

During this summer, one of our chiefs, John Sunday, with several others, departed from Rice Lake, for the west, with a design to preach to the Ojebwas. When they returned, they told us that the Indians were very eager to hear the word of God, and that many had been converted. John Sunday informed us of a certain Indian, who was so much opposed to the meetings, that he confined his wife and children to one of the islands, to prevent her attending them. But this poor woman was so anxious to obey God in attendance on worship, that she was in the habit of fording the river every night, and carrying her children on her back. Her husband was afterwards converted. He mentioned also an instance of an Indian who brought his medicine sack with him to the meeting, but on being converted, he scattered its contents to the four winds of heaven. These sacks were held very sacred among the Indians. He spoke likewise of the conversion of many chiefs, and of the flocks of children anxious to hear the word of God. He left such an impression on my mind, that often, while alone, I prayed that God might send me to instruct the children in the truths of religion.

I joined my father's class meeting; and as often as possible, I attended school during the period of two years. In June, 1834, our white missionary, Daniel McMullen, received a letter from the Rev. Wm. Case, in which it was stated that a letter had been sent to him by the Rev. John Clark, who was then the Superintendent of the missions on Lake Superior. The Superintendent requested that two native preachers and two native teachers should be sent to him. John Johnson and I, were told that we were to accompany Brothers John Taunchey and Caubage to Lake Superior, to aid Brother Clark.

Brother Caubage, and my cousin Johnson, took their departure. John Taunchey hesitated about going, because I was undecided, and my father felt unwilling at first to let me go.

One day I determined to leave the village so as to avoid going to Lake Superior; I hunted along the River Trent, hoping that John Taunchey would be gone before my return; I felt very unwilling to go. I was absent over two weeks; they were the longest two weeks I had ever experienced. Yet the whole time I felt dissatisfied; something seemed to whisper to me "George, go home, and go to Lake Superior with your uncle John Taunchey." I returned to the village. The first person I saw, informed me that my uncle was waiting for me, and that my father had left it to me to decide whether to go or to stay. Here I was; the missionaries came, and said, "George, your father has left it with you to go or stay. It is your duty to go; John is waiting, and today you must conclude." Our school mistress, Miss Pinney, came and reasoned with me. I recollected too, that I had prayed that God might prepare me to be useful to my brethren; and now, that I have some good reason to think that my prayers had been heard, and still to refuse to go, would perhaps be acting in opposition to the indications of God. I wept and prayed; but O! that night of struggle! I could not sleep. In the morning, I said to my father, "I have concluded to go, prepare me for my journey." That morning we were prepared; and on the 16th July, 1834, about noon, we were on the shore. The canoe was ready; many of the Indians prayed with us on the beach. After shaking hands with my father and the rest, we bid farewell to all we loved so tenderly. We went on board the steamboat Great Britain at Cobourg, and arrived at Toronto the next day. On the 19th of July, we saw at Toronto, on the top of one of the houses, Mr. William Lyon McKenzie, who created so much trouble in Canada in the years 1837 and 1838. He was then in the height of his popularity. He was placed upon the top of a house by his friends, in company with another lawyer, with a large gold medal around his neck. There was a large concourse of his friends who had come from Hamilton for the express purpose of seeing and cheering him. On the 20th July we left in the stage for Holland Landing; here we remained two days, for the want of a conveyance to the Snake Island Mission. At this island we tarried the whole of the Sabbath with the Indians; and had some glorious meetings. They conveyed us to the Narrows Mission. In crossing from Narrows to Cold Water Mission, we were obliged to carry our trunks on our backs. About 11 o'clock we met two runaway horses on the road to Narrows. We caught them, tied our trunks on their backs, and lead them back to Cold Water. Thus we were relieved of our heavy loads.

On Wednesday, the 26th July, we went from Cold Water Mission to Pane-ta-wa-go-shene, where we saw a great number of Ojebwas from Lake Superior, Ottawas, Menomenese, &c. Here we fell in with John Sunday, Frazer, and others, who were engaged in instructing the Indians in this vicinity.

An opportunity occurred now to go to Sault St. Marie, where the Rev. John Clark resided. We were out of provisions several times. By fishing and shooting gulls on our way, we were enabled to reach the Sault, where we met Brother Clark, John Caubage, and cousin Johnson; this took place, I believe, on the 24th of August. We stayed here about two weeks, preparing to go to the Aunce, the Ke-wa-we-non Mission. During our delay in this place, the Rev. Messrs. Chandler, and Bourne (the latter a member of the Illinois Conference, arrived. Brother Chandler has since died. My cousin, H. P. Chase, was Brother Clark's interpreter. The Indians were comfortable in their new houses. We held meeting with them several nights.

Pah-we-ting with its fisheries. Thomas Shaw, a warm and open hearted half-bred Frenchman, was in the habit of scooping out of the rapids, twenty or thirty fine white fish, and boiling them for his friends.

X

I now began to feel the responsibilities resting upon me. The thought of assuming the station of a teacher of the Indians, with so few capabilities, was enough to discourage more gifted men than myself. Frequently did I enter the woods and pour out my soul to God, in agony and tears. I trembled at what was before me; and said, "who is able for these things?" But a still small voice would answer, "My grace is sufficient for you." Soothing words indeed, especially to an unlearned and feeble Red man—a mere worm of the dust.

Having provided every thing necessary for our journey, and a residence of eight months at the Ka-wa-we-non Mission, we started in company with Rev. Mr. Chandler, uncle John Taunchey, and the traders who intended to winter on the shores of Lake Superior and do business with the Ojebwas. We were more than three weeks on our journey— three hundred and fifty miles. At one place we were weather-bound for one week. Our French companions were the most wicked of men. They would gnash their teeth at each other, curse, swear, and fight among themselves. The boat, oars, the winds, water, the teachers, etc., did not escape their execrations. I thought now that I understood what *hell* was in a very clear manner. My very hairs seemed to "stand erect like quills upon a fretful porcupine," when they gave vent to their malevolence and passions. They would fight like beasts over their cooking utensils, and even while their food was in their mouths. I will just say here that I have often seen them eat boiled corn with tallow for butter.

On our road, we saw the celebrated Pictured Rocks, Sand Banks, and Grand Island. On a point of the latter place we encamped. Every Sabbath I devoted about one hour in sighing and crying after *home*. What good can *I do*, when I reach the place of labor? was a question that often occurred to my mind. Still we were going farther and farther from home. We were obliged too, to do our own cooking, washing, and mending.

At last, in September, we arrived at the Aunce Bay. Here, our house was no better than a wigwam; and yet we had to occupy it as a dwelling, a school house, a meeting house, and a council room.

We commenced laboring among our poor people, and those that had been christianized, were exceedingly glad to see us. Brothers Sunday and Frazer had already been among them more than a year. We

GEORGE COPWAY

began to build quite late in the fall, and although we removed a house from the other side of the bay, yet we experienced much inconvenience. We visited the Indians daily, for the purpose of conversing and praying with them. There were about thirty, who had, for more than a year, professed to experience a change of heart. As my uncle was experienced in conversing with the unconverted, I endeavored to pursue his course in this respect. Each day we took a different direction in visiting the unconverted. We would sing, read the scriptures, and then pray with them. Sometimes they would be impudent, and even abusive, but this did not discourage us, or deter us from our duty. By persevering, we soon discovered that the Lord was about to bless our efforts. While my uncle was visiting some four or five wigwams, I was visiting as many others; their wigwams being near us. Our influence, with God's blessing, was now felt among them. Singing and praying were their constant employment; and some of them seemed to know nothing else but the enjoyment of the truth of the gospel, and that God can and does "forgive sin." They became the happiest of beings; their very souls were like an escaped bird, whose glad wings had saved it from danger and death. Brother Chandler preached twice every Sabbath, and taught school every other week. One Sabbath, in January, 1835, Brother Chandler preached from these words, *"And they were all filled with the Holy Ghost."* He spoke with unusual liberty; I caught some of the *same fire* with which the sermon was delivered; and interpreted it with much ardor. O what a melting season it was! The anxious and expressive looks of the Indians; the tears streaming down their cheeks, all tended to add to the occasion. My readers, here was comfort; here was one bright spot, at least, in my checkered life, that I never can forget. My poor brethren appeared to swallow every word of the sermon as I interpreted it. One John Southwind, who had been notoriously cruel and revengeful, was among the humblest and the happiest. He had been a great *Conjurer*.

On Sabbath evenings, every converted Indian would try to induce his relatives to embrace religion, and pray in the wigwams of their unconverted relatives. These happy scenes often made me forget home.

Many of the unconverted, were very revengeful; but we let them expend their vengeance on the air. One of them, *Kah-be-wah-be-ko-kay*, i.e. Spear Maker, threatened to tomahawk us, if we should come to his wigwam "with the white man's religion;" "for," said he, "already some of my family are very sick and crazy." Notwithstanding this threat, we commenced our visits, and with no other weapon than a little calico bag containing our Testament and Hymn Book. Whenever he saw us near his wigwam (we were obliged to pass near his in visiting other wigwams), he would run out, and grumble and growl like a bear escaping from its den for life. In this way we continued our visits, and had opportunities to converse with the family, which resulted in the conversion of all his children. In the month of February, he himself came to us, and plead earnestly for our forgiveness. He had gone out to hunt the Martin, with his youngest daughter, who was about ten years old. While her father was preparing a martin trap, or dead-fall, as it is sometimes called, the daughter slipped behind a tree, knelt in the snow, and prayed for her father. The Lord heard her prayer. The old man "felt sick in his heart," and every thing he looked at, appeared to frown upon him, and to bid him "go to the missionaries, and they will tell you how you can be cured." He returned home three days earlier than he had intended. Just after day-dawn, we heard a number of Indians praying. John Southwind came in and said to us, "*Ke-ge-ke-wa-ye-wah, Kak-be-wah-be-koo-bay ke-che-ah-koo-sey,*" i.e. Your friend *Spear Maker* is very sick; he wishes you to call at his wigwam and pray with him. This was good news indeed! We went at once, and prayed with him. He could not speak; but sat sobbing and sighing over the fire. We conversed with him, and then left him; but before breakfast he entered our house with his large medicine sack containing little gods of almost every description. He stood before us, and said, "*Ah bay, ah was ah yah mook,*"—here, take this. He cast the bag, or sack, down upon the floor, and wept and sobbed bitterly, saying, "I have done all I could against you, but you have been my friends. I want you to pray for me, and to burn these gods, or throw them where I can never see them." Shortly after this interview, he obtained religion, and became truly happy in the Lord.

There were many equally interesting conversions about this time. I must here mention what was often very amusing to the missionaries, and would often create a smile, if nothing more. When some of the Indians were under *conviction*, they would take some of their own medicines (herbs) to cure their "sickness,"—for so they termed *conviction*. An old medicine man once sent a message to us, stating that his daughter was dying; and that it was caused by our singing and praying before her so much; he also added, that in the event of her death, he would have his revenge by killing us, and insisted upon it, that we must come immediately, and endeavor to relieve her. We went, and after having prayed with her for some time, she revived, and expressed her confidence that the Holy Spirit had operated upon her heart. The old man soon became convinced that his daughter was not dying, except unto *sin;* he, therefore, at once, became reconciled and delighted too.

We now commenced traveling on snow shoes within fifteen or twenty miles around, where the Indians were hunting, praying, and preaching to them. The Lord owned and blessed our labors wherever we went. We held prayer meetings in the woods. All this time the *Mah-je Mon-e-doo* (Bad Spirit) was not asleep. In the spring the Heathen party started in a body to visit their old friend *Spear Maker*, for the purpose of uniting with him in dancing, and in their medicine worship; but the old man had too much religion in him to gratify them. As soon as they discovered that they could not prevail upon the old man, they sent word to all, that they could excel us in worshiping the Great Spirit; and that they intended to hold their regular spring Grand Medicine Worship. Every night we held meetings. They commenced with their *paw-wahs* (singing), and beating of the drums on the other side of the bay, and continued it for a whole week. We kept up our usual meetings; and at the end of the week, their drumming, singing, and dancing ceased. We continued our meetings for two months. The Chief of this place, was yet unconverted.

During this spring, Brother Clark, our Superintendent, arrived from the Sault St. Marie, with Brother William Herkimer and family, and my cousin Johnson. These were to take our places in the Mission. We had now an excellent quarterly meeting. Brother Clark preached a sensible and warm sermon; my cousin interpreted it. It was a blessed time; over twenty were baptised before the services began. There was a circumstance which rendered the occasion peculiarly interesting; an old Indian woman of about eighty years, came crawling to the meeting, for she was unable to walk; her name was Anna. The year before, she had traveled three hundred and fifty miles in a canoe, to be baptised by Brother Clark. She now lived about two miles from our Mission, and on the Sabbath, was brought to meeting in a canoe. But on this Sabbath, the wind was so high that no canoe could be launched. In the morning, after the others had left, she started for meeting, and crawled over logs, through creeks, and other difficult places near the edges of rocks. Old Anna made her appearance in the house, to the astonishment as well as to the delight of all. She seated herself in front of the preacher, and listened attentively to the words of eternal life. She united with others in praising God for his mercy and goodness, especially to herself. She then partook of the body and blood of her Saviour. She spoke of the day in which she was in darkness; but now she knew, by experience, that the Lord had forgiven her sins. She cared not for the *water, mud,* or *precipices*, if she could only crawl or creep to meeting, for she felt well rewarded, because the Lord blessed her. She did not, like some, fear to soil her clothes; neither was she a *fair day visitor* of meeting. Before her conversion, she was a celebrated conjurer, and a dread to the nation; every one was afraid to incur her displeasure. The last time I saw her, was in 1842, and she was still confiding in the Lord.

We were now to accompany Brother Clark to St. Marie. We started on Tuesday afternoon at about three o'clock, in our large bark canoe, which was about thirty-six feet long, five feet wide in the centre, and three feet high. We paddled about nine miles. On the next morning, we hoisted our sail before a fresh breeze and sailed at the rate of nine knots an hour. We reached the point on the Sand Banks in the evening, having previously tarried three hours with the Indians at Grand Island. The next day we sailed about six miles from the shore; it was quite boisterous; and when in the trough of the wave it was impossible for us to see the land. We now came within a few miles of White-fish Point. On the following day we hoisted our sail again, and had a favorable wind; we went down the Falls of St. Marie in handsome style, about twelve o'clock. *Waub-ke-newh** (White Eagle) walked about Sault St. Marie attending to the interests of the Missions. He was the theme of conversation in every circle, for none had ever traveled the distance in so short a time. The traders were much surprised. The Indians could hardly think it possible for any person to travel the distance in so short a time.

Note.—On our way to St. Marie, we saw that one of the Points of Grand Island had sunk. It was formed of quicksand. It was told to the trader, Charles Holiday, by the Indians, that the Great Spirit had removed from under that point to some other place, because the Methodist Missionaries had encamped there the previous fall, and had, by their *prayers* driven the Spirit from under the point. They did not wish the missionaries to encamp any where on their Island again, fearing that the Island would sink.

---

* This was the name given by my poor brethren to Brother Clark, and a more appropriate one could not have been given.—*The King of Birds.* They knew that he had come to be instrumental in saving their never dying souls.

XI

We spent a few weeks at the Sault with the brethren, with whom we had some precious seasons. We were soon informed by our beloved Superintendent that three of us would have to go to Ottawa Lake:—Taunchey, Marksman, and myself. We had, as was supposed, provisions enough to last till we reached La Pointe, where we were to obtain a fresh supply for seven months. Brothers *Tah-yash*, and *Ma-mah-skah-wash* i.e. *Fast-sailer*, accompanied us. We had a new canoe, good oars, and a new sail. After leaving, the first place which we arrived at was about six miles above the Sault St. Marie. We here saw a porcupine on the beach; and having beat it to death, we cooked and ate it for supper. After this we were wind-bound for several days, which delayed our arrival at the Ke-wa-we-non Mission, on our way to La Pointe. On entering Aunce Bay, we were in much danger. The wind rose, with a dense fog accompanying it, and we were without a compass. We steered our course by the wind. We were very near being dashed to pieces against a large rock a few feet from us, which we espied just in time to avoid. I had been on Lake Superior, but never saw the waves run so high as on the present occasion. It was truly wonderful that our bark canoe stood the sea so well. Nor could we see any prospect of landing. Still the spray of the gigantic waves continued to roll after us in terrific fury. The canoe still struggled between the mountain waves, and then would rise on the top. The sail spread itself like a duck just ready to fly. It appeared at times that we must all perish. But God was with us. O how kind and merciful is that Being who has the winds and waves in his hands! "O Lord *I will* praise thee," etc. It is religion alone that can support in time of danger. Faith lays hold on God. Yes, let *distress, sickness, trials, perils*, and even *death* come, yet if in thy hands, O Lord, we are secure.

Through a kind providence, we arrived at last at Brother Herkimer's, about ten o'clock, A.M. How we surprised them when they were told that we sailed all the morning through the fog. They at once saw the danger; but we could take no other course. We remained here but a few days. On Tuesday, we left for La Pointe, one hundred and sixty miles. Here was another tedious journey, for we were again wind-bound for three days; in consequence of this misfortune our provisions were exhausted. We went to Ah-too-nah-kun River on Friday evening, and traveled all night to reach Porcupine Mountains, where we arrived at day light. We stepped out of the canoe, took our blankets, wrapped them around us, and lay on the solid rocks, where we slept about an hour and a half. Saturday morning arrived, and found us with nothing but half a pound of tea; we were now eighty-eight miles from La Pointe. We rowed all the morning, when a favorable breeze sprung up, which enabled us to gain fifty miles during that day. After nightfall we toiled to reach La Pointe by twelve o'clock on Saturday night; but we were so fatigued, sleepy, and hungry, that it was impossible to continue rowing. Now and then a little land-breeze would help us along slowly, without rowing. At last we were obliged to give up rowing, as the oars were dragging in the water. I steered the boat as well as I could. We labored hard to keep awake. I thought of the tea; I chewed a mouthful of it and swallowed the juice; but in a few minutes I suffered so much from a griping pain that I was alarmed. Oh I was miserable, sick, and hungry. I could not wake any of the company; and when my pain ceased, I could scarcely keep myself awake. I now steered for the shore; it was about twelve o'clock. I threw my blanket around me, and left all hands sleeping in the boat. I threw up a little bank of sand for a pillow, and the soft wet sand was my bed. I was soon in the land of *Nod*.

Sabbath morning came. I had dreamed that we were just about sitting down to a warm breakfast, when Peter Marksman awoke me, and said, "George, come, get up, *blackfast* (breakfast, he meant, he could speak but little English). If it had not been the Sabbath, I might have been induced to retaliate. It was indeed, a *blackfast*, dark enough; nothing to eat, and only tea to drink for breakfast, dinner and supper! and yet, only about fiften miles from La Pointe; indeed, we could *see* the place; and had it not been that it was the Sabbath, feeble as we were, we would have proceed. Here, then, we spent the Sabbath. I walked into the woods, and all that I could think of while reading my Bible, was *home*. I looked towards *home*, and wept at the thought of it. I said to myself, O my father, if you knew my situation today, you would feel for me, and fly, if possible, to assist me! I feel that your prayers ascend for me; and then descend like gentle rains, into my soul. *Home! home!* however humble, it is still *home*. This day, however, is a glorious day for my soul; but how insupportable for the body! We had a prayer meeting in the evening, which is still as fresh in my grateful memory as if it had but just taken place.

GEORGE COPWAY

Monday morning, before the sun arose, we were on our way to La Pointe, where we arrived about ten o'clock. Mr. Warren, the trader at this place, supplied us with some necessaries. We breakfasted with him, and never did fish and potatoes taste half so sweet as now.

We called on the Rev. Mr. Hall, and others of the Presbyterian Mission. How kindly they received and entertained us; they compelled us to live in their families, while we remained in that place. We had now to prepare to depart for Ottawa Lake, where we had been appointed by Brother Clark to spend the winter, in teaching the Indians. O what a field for labor in all these regions! Indians, from every direction, congregate here every summer; those, too, who have never heard of a Saviour!

When will all my poor people "sit together in heavenly places in Christ Jesus"? When will they cease to offer up to the Bad Spirit all they possess? Shall these also perish as did the Indians on the eastern coast? The red men of the forest were then unconscious that the white man would at some future day, spread his white sails on these waters, and claim their native woods; that a steamboat would make its appearance, like a monster from the deep, snorting *fire* and *smoke*, near their shores. God of mercy, save, save my poor people.

We started for the Ottawa Lake about the eighth of October, 1835. We had to carry our canoes, with the rest of our articles, over eight portages, or carrying places, one of which was nine, and another five miles long. No language can convey an idea of the hardships and toil to which we were exposed, before we reached there; for we had to carry all our things over the carrying places; and as it was too late in the fall, and on account of the disagreeableness of the weather, we were obliged to return to La Pointe. The winter set in, and we traveled one hundred and seventy miles by land. It was on one of these carrying places that I carried the heavy load mentioned on page 19.

When we arrived at Ottawa Lake, the Indians were glad to see us. The Chief, Moose Ogeed, *Moose tail*, was particularly kind. Here we labored with success, though at the time many of them were absent hunting. I commenced a day-school with few scholars. During the winter our provisions gave out; for seven weeks we had nothing, except what we caught by spearing and shooting; but in the latter part of the winter we could neither shoot rabbits, nor spear fish. What now was to be done, except to go to La Pointe, one hundred and seventy miles, and obtain some flour. We ran nearly all day through the woods, and the next day my feet were blistered, occasioned by the strap of my snow shoes. The young man who accompanied me, suffered still more, for the blood was oozing out through his moccasons. At the expiration of two days, at about ten o'clock in the morning, we were at Rev. Mr. Hall's, at La Pointe. Brother Hall could hardly credit the fact that we had walked one hundred and seventy miles in *less* that two days.

On returning to the mission, we were one week on our journey. I had over seventy pounds of provisions to carry when I left, and my friend and companion, whom I hired, had eighty-five pounds. The Indians too were almost starving; but the spring opened just in time to save them. In their journey, down the river, we accompanied them, and had an opportunity to converse with them about religion. On our way, the Indians pointed to the battle grounds of the Ojebwas and the Sioux. How dreadful and awful was their description. The Chief, pointing to a certain spot, observed, "There I killed two Sioux, about thirteen winters ago; I cut open one of them; and when I reflected that the Sioux had cut up my own cousin, but a year before, I took out his heart, cut a piece from it, and swallowed it whole. I scooped some of his blood, while warm, with my hand, and drank as many draughts as the number of friends who had perished by their hands." As he spoke, the fierceness of the Indian gleamed from his countenance. Every half mile, trees were blazed (barked), and notches made according to the number that had been killed.

The Sioux and the Ojebwas have been at war from time immemorial. The neutral ground of these two nations, is full of game, such as deer, bears, elks, etc. We went down to the Me-no-me-nee Mills, on the Chippewa River, where the whites were cutting down pine trees. We then returned to Ottawa Lake, and, afterwards, to La Pointe.

During this winter I was with the Rev. Mr. Hall, at La Pointe, and assisted him in translating the Gospel of St. Luke, and the Acts of the Apostles, into the Ojebwa tongue. Although I have sat hour after hour in assisting him in his good work in the west, yet I can never, never repay him for the kindness and affection shown to me. May God reward him for his labors of love, and for his Christian benevolence. He is like a pure and limpid stream which is ever running, and which never dries up. He is like a high rock on the sea shore, when the storms and waves have passed by, unchanging and unchanged. He is in all respects the most suitable man for this work, being devoted, humble, kind, affectionate, and benevolent, and is master of our language. I hope to see him once, if not many times, more, that I may thank him again and again for his Christian goodness. May his holy and arduous life, and health, be precious in God's sight.

Here I must make a remark. In that country, we ought not to know each other as Presbyterians, Methodists, or Baptists, but only as missionaries of the cross. We should labor with and for each other; and do all the good we can. Our language should always be, "come brethren, let us labor side by side, hold up each others hands in the work, share each others trials and privations; and spread the gospel of the blessed God." May many Brother Halls be raised up for these stations; so that the poor outcast red man, may soon take his station among Christians of every civilized clime. Should these observations fall under the eye of dear Brother Hall, he will, I am sure, forgive me for the warm and candid confessions of a sincere heart.

XII

We spent part of the summer at La Pointe, waiting for our Superintendent, Rev. John Clark, who intended to go by the way of Ottawa Lake down the Mississippi. He arrived the latter part of June, with his companions. We went in two canoes up *Bad River*, and thence over the Portages, already named. We divided our provisions, bedding, etc., etc., so that each should carry an equal weight. In ascending Bad River we were nearly half of the time in the water, draging the canoe up the stream. One day Brother Clark stepped on a rock above the water, in the centre of the river, for the purpose of holding the canoe while those that were exceedingly tired, might rest. As soon as he had put his foot on the rock, the canoe wheeled around with the current, which drew him into it, and carried him down the river. We were alarmed for some time, and it was with the greatest efforts that we could save him. At times, we could only see his white hat above the water. At first, we could not render him the least assistance. The stream conveyed him near the shore, where he seized the limb of a tree, which enabled him to reach land. We hurried to the spot where he landed, jumped out of the canoe, and ran after him, but before we could see him, we heard him cry out "*whoop*," and in a few moments saw him coming through the leaves soaking wet. We were all thankful indeed to see him alive, and so cheerful too. On that day we would not permit him to carry but two loads or packs, the others carried three. Our wish was that he should not *at any time* carry *any thing;* but he insisted upon helping us, and to this we had to submit. This was one of those kind traits which endeared him so much to all his fellow laborers. He has also shared the last morsel of bread with us. Often has he carried the canoe on his back; and when we were discouraged and faint, he would encourage us by his cheerful countenance, and words of consolation. Our sinking hearts have often been made to beat with emotions of joy; for during these journeys we had ample reasons and time for desponding. But according to our trials, did we enjoy the smiles of heaven.

We were three days going over the Nine Mile Portage, where we spent the Sabbath. We had three loads each; and the two canoes were also to be carried, each one taking his turn every half mile. We were now completely jaded out; our bones ached. This was the hardest journey that I ever made, with the exception of the one which will hereafter be related.

After severe toil and privations, we arrived at Ottawa Lake, where Brother Clark met the chief and some of his warriors in council. He explained the object of our visit, viz. to live among them and teach them; to which the chief assented.

Brother Clark now left Johnson, Marksman, and myself here, to do all the good we could. On departing, we accompanied him down the river for two days; and on the first of August we bade each other farewell.

That day, Peter and John were inconsolable, because Brother Clark and the rest had left us for a whole year. I felt so "choked up" and deserted, that I talked but little during the day. After praying, as Brother Clark was parting with us, and our heads were resting on the canoe, he said, "Brethren, take courage; do all the good you can. Pray much; trust in God; tell the Indians how the Saviour died; we will pray for you; good bye; and may the Lord bless you and your labors."

We returned to Ottawa Lake, and built a house, where we resided during the year. Quite late in the fall, Johnson and Marksman left me, and went to La Pointe, where they remained all the winter. It is true, there were but few Indians here, but yet, too many for one teacher. They wished me to go with them, but I preferred, from a sense of duty, to spend the winter and spring in teaching, singing, and praying among the people here. In the spring an interesting conversion took place; the convert committed the fourteenth chapter of St. John before he had learned the alphabet. This young man had been remarkably kind, and humane, before his conversion; he was more like a Christian than any unconverted man I ever saw. I never heard any thing proceed from his mouth that was censurable. One Sabbath morning, while we were in the woods, I was reading to him, "God so loved the world, that he gave his only begotten Son, that whosoever believeth on him, might not perish, but have everlasting life." This was like an arrow in his heart; he prayed, and wrestled with God, until the Lord spoke peace to his soul.

In the summer, when Johnson and Marksman arrived, John and I went down to Prairie Du Chien, on the Mississippi. On our way, we had to pass through the land of the Sioux, the enemies of the Ojebwas, and we knew not what would be our fate. However, we pursued our course and ventured at their village. As soon as we approached, they raised the war-whoop and fired some guns over our heads, and the bullets either splashed in front of our canoe, or whizzed about our heads. Still, we kept on our course, and as soon as we stepped from our canoe, they seized us, and kept us prisoners for nearly three days. When we told them (through an interpreter) that we were missionaries, they released us, and treated us kindly. On the third day we were on the water again, on our way to Prairie Du Chien, which place we reached, and there saw Brother Brunson, the Superintendent for that year. We accompanied him to St. Peters, near the Falls of St. Anthony; and the same summer, through the kindness of Brother Clark, we were sent to school near Jacksonville, Illinois. To Brother Clark, under God, I owe all the education (little as it is) which I now possess. Before this, I could neither speak nor read five words correctly. Brothers Johnson, Marksman, and myself, were placed under the care of the Rev. Jno. Mitchell, now an assistant at the Book Concern, in Cincinnatti. For two years we attended school at the Ebenezer Seminary, about two miles north of Jacksonville. At this institution, I passed some of the happiest seasons of my life. Many who were with me at this school, are now ministers of the Gospel, both among the whites and the Indians. The groves seemed vocal with the praises of God. The camp meeting, and the quarterly meetings, which I then attended, are still fresh in my memory. The remembrance of the many delightful acquaintances formed, the appointments filled, the interesting meetings I attended in different parts, about Jacksonville, at Lynville, Manchester, Rushville, and Versailes, will always hold a seat in my heart. It was here that I learned to read the word of God, and often, for hours together, upon my knees, in the groves, have I been thus engaged. O the sweet communion I then had with God!

Among the many letters which I have since received from my schoolmates, I will trouble the reader only with the following:—

MT. STERLING, *Brown Co., Ill.*}
February 8th, 1845.}

DEAR BROTHER COPWAY,

With pleasure I improve this privilege of answering your kind epistle, and taking a "paper talk" with you. By the blessings of the good Lord, we are well. But I hear you say "What does he mean by *we?*"—Only myself, my wife, and boy! Now if you will pardon me this time for marrying young, I will promise never to do so again. But I think you will not be severe in your censure, inasmuch as I have a worthy precedent in you. Brother Troy traveled three years, and married Brother Stratten's daughter, of Pike county; and I, who commenced three years after him, preached two years, and married another; so we, who had long been brothers, became brothers-in-law. Brother Wm. Piper was married since conference, to Squire Baynes' daughter, near Columbus. Harden Wallace married Miss Bronson, of Athens, one year since. Brother S. Spates is on a visit to his friends, and has the ague; neither he nor Reason is married, but have "good desires." I visited Brother George, two weeks since.

We have glorious times in religion. O it would have done you good to have heard Dr. Akers tell his experience, in our last quarterly meeting. In speaking of his sanctification he said, with a peculiar emphasis, while his lips trembled and tears filled his eyes, *It was the revelation of the Son of God in me.* But time would fail to tell of these "Ebenezer" boys, who through faith, preach "big sermons," exhort thousands, "who are valiant in fight," who slaughter many a sinner, and wear the marks of many a well fought field, although death has done his work among us! Our faithful teacher, and a beloved schoolmate, Brothers Troy and Piper, are no more; they fell victims to fever just after conference; but they fell like martyrs, they died at their post. Brother Troy and I, attended Bro. Piper's funeral (the sermon was preached by Brother Berryman) at Barry. It was a solemn time. While I stood by his coffin, I thought of you all, and of Brother *Huddlestun*, who had gone before him. The day before I left, Father Stratten, Brother Troy, and I, walked out on the Mississippi bluffs, while the bright surface of the river reflected upon us the last rays of the setting sun. We talked of the happy days of other years, spent with kindred spirits now scattered over the world. His breast seemed warmed at the recollection. The flame of his zeal mounted high, and pointing to the bright waters that rolled in the distance, he said, "I feel like preaching till the last sinner on the last tributary of that stream is converted to God." Alas! he had even then preached his last sermon. Peace to their memory. "They taught us how to *live*, and O how high the price of knowledge, taught us how to *die.*" Sister Piper, and her two children, live at her own home in Barry; Sister Troy, with one child, lives with her father. You have, perhaps, read the obituaries of Brothers Benson, Otwell, Corey, Edmunson, and Hale—gone home. Brother N. W. Allen, married down south, and John Mathers to Miss Julia Tucker. Brother Heddenburg is in Springfield. I believe M. has concluded not to marry, but to keep house for her father. Moses C. lives and prospers in Petersburgh Circuit.

March 13*th.* I commence again, not having time to finish when I commenced. I record with sorrow the death of our child, aged eight months. The affliction of one short week, carried him beyond the sorrows incident to mortality, to rest with God. O it was a trial to see him sink in death, and bear him to the grave. But now, thank God,

> "The storm that wrecks the winter sky,
> No more disturbs his sweet repose,
> Than summer evening's latest sigh,
> That shuts the rose."

The Lord has given us some tokens for good; we have some glorious prayer and class meetings. Thirteen joined on my last round. I expect Brother Wallace with me at a protracted meeting next week; can you not come too?

Well, Brother George, how do you get along in religion? This is the subject *all important.* Time, in its rapid roll, still bears us on. The sun stood still in Gibeon, but time did not stand still. The sun went back ten degrees on the dial of Ahaz, but time rolled on with unremitting speed. *Mutation* is written all around us. The little flower, so bright, is nipped by the untimely frost of winter. The rainbow is beautiful, but it passes away with the weeping cloud. And O how soon the fleeting years of time will be lost amid the mighty cycles of eternity. And yet, my brother, we know that on this inch of time hang everlasting things. Lord, help us to stamp every moment with improvement. Now, if God has entrusted to us the care of souls immortal, how should we pray and labor, lest we should lose a prize so dear!

Brother George, I shall never forget our band society, and "young men's" prayer meeting; these were precious seasons.

Though I view my brethren falling round me, the hope of immortality makes "the valley of the shadow" flame with the glory of God. Thank God for religion that can conquer death, and view the grave as but a subterranean passage to the skies. Go on—I expect to hail you in a better clime. Brother, I think I have *experienced* that the *blood of Christ cleanseth from all sin.* O glorious truth! Have you not found it too? It is by simple *Faith.*

> *"Faith has an eye no tears can dim;*
> *A heart no griefs can stir.*
> *She bears the cross, and looks to Him*
> *Who bore the cross for her."*

Go on, brother; the land of rest lies just across the rolling tide of Jordan. Methinks I see a Troy, a Huddlestun, and Piper, put forth their hands from the banks of glory, to beckon us onward. They look out for us; O let us not disappoint them! You know the north and south talk of division; thank God they can't divide me, nor break those ties that bind me to good brethren every where, from whom "joy, nor grief, nor time, nor place, nor life, nor death, can part."

I must close my scattering letter, though not half done. Brother come down, and I'll try and tell you the rest. We can go over to Ebenezer and have a meeting. Pitner is there now. He says that the Lord has the best market in the universe; christian duties are always good sale there, and then we are sure to get a "back load" of grace. He says, "the Lord has a great big two-story *ware-house:* the promise of the life that now is, that's the *lower* story; and of that which is to come, this is the *upper* story. There," says he, "brethren, I'll not tell you any more, you'll have to die to know the rest."

My very best respects to your lady, and the little Copways.

Yours, fraternally,

WILLIAM J. RUTLEDGE

N. B. Dr. Vandevanter, Brother Bond, and many others, still speak of your preaching at Versailes. We have some good times there now. Brothers Billy and Cabble Patterson are married; yes, and Aquilla too. He preaches, and teaches school. Brothers Saxon still goes it with a rush. The "first year" class of boys in this conference, are now first rate; some of them could almost stride a mountain. O sir, it would do you good to see Brother Billy Piper throw his searing thunderbolts and rive the forest oak, or bury them in the smoking earth. See him rise in the fulness of his strength, and exclaim, "Man fell; Heaven was robed in silence, Earth in sorrow, and Hell alone was glad." Farewell.

W. J. R.

I attended several of the Conferences; the last of which was in Bloomfield, in 1839, where I parted with some of my dearest friends and companions, for nine months. Still it was pleasant to reflect that the Conference had appointed Brothers Spates, Huddleston, Johnson, and Peter Marksman, to labor at the head of the Mississippi. Brother Kavanaugh was appointed Superintendent of the Missions for that year. I was allowed to visit home in the fall, to see my friends. I traveled to Chicago free of expense; I drove a pair of fine grey horses for an individual who was on his road to that place. We slept in our wagons every night. At Chicago* I embarked in a schooner for Buffalo; but getting tired of this, left it at Detroit, and took steamboat for Buffalo, where I arrived just about day light. I had lost my cap, the wind blew it into the lake, with my pocket-book, containing $27 in bills, and $2.50 in silver, with a silk handkerchief, in which my all was wrapped. Here I was, moneyless, friendless, and hatless, and in a strange land! I had, however, a little change left. I had made up my mind to visit the East before my return to Canada. But this must now be abandoned. I walked about Buffalo quite disheartened. At last I saw on a sign "Temperance Hotel." I concluded to put up at this house, and to my surprise and joy, the landlord was a warm hearted Methodist—James Madison. At night, I accompanied him to the prayer meeting, where he told a Brother Copeland my circumstances. They made up the whole amount of my loss, and gave me a dollar over. I could now visit the East as I had purposed before my loss. The next day I started for Rochester, where I spent the Sabbath. I was very anxious to see the great cities of which I had read so much at school. I resolved to go through thick

---

* Chicago signifies *the place of skunks*.

and thin for the sake of seeing New York. At Rochester I stopped with Brother Colby; Miss Colby perceiving that I was not warmly clad, gave me a cloak which she obtained from Brother S. Richardson. Should either, or both, of these dear friends see these remarks concerning their kindness, I hope they will excuse me for thus mentioning their names. I must thank them again for their goodness; I often remember them in my closet and by the wayside. May God reward them, and all other friends.

On Monday, I left for Albany. When I reached Syracuse, I took the long-looked for rail road. We were soon on our way, moving along like a streak of lightning. In the morning I arrived in Albany in time for the morning boat for New York. I walked around this Dutch city; and as every thing appeared to be somewhat new, I was interested, especially with the vessels, &c. As I wished to be economical, I left without any breakfast. I was charmed with the steamboat. We passed down the Hudson; the towns, villages, and the splendid scenery enchanted me. I had seen but very few such magnificent scenes before.

About noon, a plain looking man approached me; I discovered at once that he was of that class of men called Quakers. He spoke of what they were doing for the Indians in New-York. I was very much interested with his conversation. I felt glad and proud to have the honor and pleasure of seeing, and conversing with one of Penn's descendants—the friend of the poor Indians. While conversing with him, the bell was rung for dinner; he wished me to go down and eat; I told him I was obliged to be saving, as I had but little money and was not accustomed to traveling. Upon saying this, he pulled out a dinner ticket from his pocket, and said, "*Friend*, thou must take this and come down to dinner." I had an exalted opinion of the Quakers before, but this kind act increased my feelings, and confirmed all that I had ever heard of their generosity to my poor people. "God bless the Quakers," said I, silently, as I descended to dinner. After dinner we finished our conversation. He said he was on his way to Philadelphia. God bless him wherever he is. He has my kindest wishes.

In the evening I arrived at New-York, and went immediately to see Brother Mason, who directed me to go to Sister Luckey's, in Broome street, where I tarried during my stay.

On the 25th of October, came that great jubilee of Methodism. In the morning I went with Dr. Bangs to meeting. He preached the centenary sermon, which was afterwards printed. In the evening I attended the Allen street Station. Oh what a happy meeting this was. Here I saw some of the greatest among them weep for joy. "Amen, halleluiah, glory to God," and similar exclamations, rang through, and filled the house. In this vast assembly was a solitary Indian—George Copway! Never can I forget that evening! Whatever may be my future lot in this life, I will always thank God for the privilege of attending these services. May the Lord pour out his Spirit on all his churches.

The next day I visited Newark, N. J., to see Brother Abraham Hedenburg, with whom I had become acquainted in Illinois, at the house of his Brother James. Here I met with a great deal of kindness. Brother Bartine, of the Franklin Station, requested me to preach for him in the morning; and Brother Ayers, of the Northern Station, invited me to preach for him in the evening. Brother Ayers gave me about $8.00 worth of books, which I had the pleasure of perusing during the winter. This was a favor—a distinguished favor indeed. I have seen that dear Brother but once since. May the Lord be gracious to him.

My visit to Brother Hedenburg was delighful. I met many friends here, to whom I can never be thankful enough. May God visit them in great mercy. I saw them again last summer, and partook of their kind hospitalities. I feel more and more indebted to them; especially to Brother Hedenburgh.

My next journey was to Boston. Dr. Bangs gave me a letter of introduction to a brother in that city. I remained about two weeks, looking at the Yankees and their city. Boston is much overrated; there are a few, very few pretty spots; the rest is crooked and narrow. It is far behind New York, Philadelphia, and perhaps Baltimore, and New Orleans. I met with a few choice spirits—Brothers King, Rand, Wise, and Smith; and on the Sabbath, I addressed the Sabbath School in Russel street. In the evening we had a delightful meeting. I remained with Brother H. Merrell's family during my sojourn, and I shall always recollect them with feelings of sincere gratitude. I visited several noted places while in that vicinage,—the Monument on Bunker's (or rather Breed's) Hill, etc.; I went also on the top of the State House when the sky was clear. It was from this point that I saw the works of the white man. The steeples, vessels arriving, and others spreading their sails for distant lands. The wharves were filled with merchandise. A few steamboats were running here and there, breathing out fire and smoke. On my left, I noticed several towns. The steam cars from Worcester rolled on from the west; others were starting for Providence, and whizzed along the flats like a troop of runaway horses. Here were factories in different directions. As I saw the prosperity of the white man, I said, while tears filled my eyes, "Happy art thou, O Israel, who is like unto thee, *O people saved by the Lord!*" When I thought of the noble race of red men who once lived and roamed in all the land, and upon the waters as far as my eye could reach, the following thoughts arose in my mind, which I have since penned.

> *Once more I see my fathers' land*
> *Upon the beach, where oceans roar;*
> *Where whiten'd bones bestrew the sand,*
> *Of some brave warrior of yore.*
> *The groves, where once my fathers roam'd—*
> *The rivers, where the beaver dwelt—*
> *The lakes, where angry waters foam'd—*
> *Their charms, with my fathers, have fled.*
>
> *O! Tell me, ye "pale faces," tell,*
> *Where have my proud ancestors gone?*
> *Whose smoke curled up from every dale,*
> *To what land have their free spirits flown?*
> *Whose wigwams stood where cities rise;*
> *On whose war-paths the steam-horse flies;*
> *And ships, like mon-e-doos in disguise,*
> *Approach the shore in endless files.*

I now visited the Missionary Rooms of the American Board, whose invaluable labors are felt throughout the globe. I saw some articles, wrought by our people in the west, such as bead work, porcupine quills, moccasons, war clubs, etc. I thought, that if Brother Greene had seen as much of war clubs as I had (for I have seen them stained with blood and notched according to the number of individuals they had slain), he would conceal them from every eye.

XIII

About the 4th of November, I took my leave of Boston, for the great commercial emporium, on my route homewards. My traveling companion was the Rev. E. Taylor, the sailor's friend. He was on his way to Philadelphia to preach. I should suppose that a better sailor's preacher cannot be found in the Union. I was much pleased with his conversation. In one of his public addresses, I was told that he said, "When I die, smother me not under the dust; but bury me in the sea, where the sea-weed will be my winding sheet, the coral my coffin, and the sea shell my tomb stone." I heard an individual say of him, "Start him where you will, he will go to sea."

I was now, once more, in the magnificent city of New-York. I bought a few books at the Book Rooms. After surveying the beauties and curiosities of the city, I left in the steamboat Rochester for Albany. I spent one day in Albany, and attended a Methodist prayer meeting. The Rev. Mr. Seymour, the preacher in charge at the Division street Station, introduced me to Brother Page, who had the charge of the South Ferry street Church. At the latter church I was present at a delightful and soul-stirring meeting.

The following day I took the canal for Syracuse and Oswego. On my way from Schenectady to Utica I preached twice on board the boat; and even here I found some pious souls. I observed the tears falling from several eyes. "The Lord be praised," was the language of my heart. When shall this poor heart, feel fully and wholly alive, to the unsurpassed favors of Heaven?

I took a steamboat at Oswego, and arrived at Kingston, C. W., on the evening of Nov. 11. Here I had to pay duties on the books which I had obtained in New-York. The amount to be paid was $32.50, and I had but $27. I went to Charles Oliver, Deputy Collector; and as soon as I laid my circumstances before him, he said, "pay the $27, and I will advance you the balance; and as soon as you reach home, write to Mr. McCauley, the Inspector General, who lives in Toronto, and inform him who you are; he will, doubtless, authorize me to refund you the money." I did so, and shortly afterwards received the whole amount. In this public way, I would express my most hearty thanks to these gentlemen for their acts of kindness towards an Indian stranger.

I arrived at Rice Lake on the 12th day of November, 1839, having been absent from home five years and four months. Never did I feel so rejoiced as when I stood on the top of a hill, and saw my village, seven miles across the lake. I gazed upon it with pure delight; and as I took a retrospective view of all the scenes which I had passed through, I wondered at myself, and at the great goodness of God. I knelt down, and "blessed and thanked Him who liveth for ever," for his unspeakable goodness to a child of sin. While crossing the lake, I was in perfect ecstacies; my heart leaped with joy; and my thoughts and emotions were at my home long before my person. Oh how tedious and tardy the boat seemed to be; I wished for wings several times. But at last, I planted my foot upon the spot on which I had been reared from my infancy, and where some of the sweetest and happiest recollections of my life were centered. But "every sweet has its bitter." On inquiring for some of my relatives, I was informed that they had left this, for a better life. Many of my old friends and acquaintances had gone to try the realities of another world. Numbers were bathed in tears, and the wounds of their hearts were re-opened. My own heart seemed to bleed at every pore. What a painful interview! I now requested to be shown the graves of my dear relatives and friends. I wended my way to these consecrated grounds, and sighed and wept over them. My reflections were solemn indeed! I followed many of them, in my thoughts, to heaven, whither they doubtless now are, celebrating the praises of God around the throne of the blessed Redeemer. This was great consolation amidst my griefs; and I now felt determined, with God's assistance, to follow them, so far as they followed Christ, and thus be prepared to unite with them in the songs of the upper world, whenever God shall see fit to call me hence.

Brother John Sunday, was at this time, stationed in our village. The Lord soon visited this Mission with a glorious revival; many were converted, and others reclaimed. The tracts that I had received at the Book Rooms, and the books from the American Tract Society (N. Y.), I distributed among those that could read, and they were duly appreciated. I believe that these were the means which prepared their minds to relinquish the world, and place their hope in God.

I will now speak of Christmas and New Year. When Christmas arrived, we were invited to a centenary tea party, in company with the Rev. William Case, the well known friend of the Indians. The party met at Alderville, eight miles from the Mission. This was a season of much joy and happiness. The Chiefs referred to the time when they were without the gospel. One of them said, "Before I heard the gospel, when Christmas came, I began to thank the Great Spirit for the day on which I could get plenty of *whiskey*. Brothers, you know how often I was dragged through the snow to my wigwam, where my wife and children were cold and hungry. Now, I drink *tea* instead of *whiskey*, and have religion with it; now my house is comfortable; and my children are pious and happy. I expect to pursue a Christian course till I arrive in heaven. My fond hope is to meet these good missionaries in the land of bliss; and not only these, but also the good John Wesley, with whom I expect to shake hands there." John Sunday's brother (Big Jacob), said, "When the Methodists were preaching to our people, I heard that the chiefs and warriors were frequently in tears. I then said, I would not shed tears were I to hear them. Still, I wished to understand for myself. I went, with a full determination not to behave myself like a *woman*, I mean by crying. I sat near the door. The preacher was speaking about the Saviour's dying on the cross, while the Indians all around were sobbing. I began to feel serious, and then the tears fell involuntarily. Frequently, I wiped my eyes, but still the tears *would flow*. I asked myself, *am I crying too?* Brethren, I was ashamed to exhibit tears; but now (here he raised his hand to heaven), it is not through cowardice that I cry, for I never shed a tear on the battle field, nor even when my children or my friends lay dead before me. No! I never dropped a tear. I feel tonight very happy and thankful to know that the Great Spirit did not, while I was in darkness, say, 'I will never bless this Indian.' I feel an ardent love for you all. I love *Jesus*, who has done so much for sinful me." He then sat down; Brother John Sunday now arose, and interpreted what his brother had just said; and at the close of his remarks, he turned to the whites, who had come here from Cobourg, and several other places, and said, "Brothers, that was a *great big mercy*, for that *great big man*."

I might add other cases here, but it is scarcely necessary. Suffice it to say that we enjoyed the services throughout. As I looked around, I recognised some, whom I knew, and had often seen before the gospel reached us, and who had usually spent Christmas in the gutter,—degraded, miserable, and starving. The language of the Psalmist might well have been quoted by each of these poor brethren:—"Thou hast raised me up out of the filthiest sink (English translation, '*the miry clay*'), and hast planted my feet firmly on a rock." Yes, the rock Christ Jesus.

New Year's day was observed in the same religious manner. And I cannot but remark here, that it is to be greatly regretted that so many Christians in the States spend this day in gadding about from house to house, and indulging in luxuries to excess. Nay, more; I have been informed that not a few professors entertain their visitors with *fire-water*, or *devil's spittle*, on that day. What a contradiction this would be in the estimation of converted Indians, were they to witness these scenes.

During the winter, the General Council of the Nation, was held at the Credit River Mission. Chief Joseph Sawyer was elected President of the Council. This noble chief has filled the chair several times since, with great credit. Several petitions, and other important documents were drawn up and signed by the different chiefs, to be presented to the Government of Canada. The whole Council waited on the Governor General, Lord Sydenham, in a body; they presented their petitions (see Note A, at the end of this chapter). In reply, we received but little satisfaction; he closed his note, by saying, "My children, for the present, I bid you all Farewell." His Lordship did not even deign to affix his *name* to the note. Since then, nothing has been heard of our papers, and therefore we must conclude that they have been laid *under* the table. But what could be expected of a "*father*," who could smile in the presence of his "*children*," and yet stab them in the dark? See Note B, at the close of the chapter, where the reader may find an extract from his letter to Lord John Russell. To rebut his false representations, I would appeal to the Report of the Commissioners on Indian Affairs in Canada; to the missionaries; and to the whole civilized and christianized population of the Chippewa nation. I can therefore say, without the fear of respectable contradiction, that his assertions have no foundation in truth. A few drunken Indians, it is true, may be found in Canada; and these alone, would be willing to call him *Father*.

It was at this General Council that I became acquainted with Captain Howell's family, of Toronto, formerly of England, and after an intimate acquaintance of some six months, I was united in marriage to his daughter Elizabeth. My wife has been a help, meet indeed; she has shared my woes, my trials, my privations; and has faithfully labored to instruct and assist the poor Indians, whenever an opportunity occurred. I often feel astonished when I reflect upon what she has endured, considering that she does not possess much physical strength. I can truly say that she has willingly partaken of the same cup that I have, although that cup has often contained *gall*. I trust, that I have not transgressed the bounds of delicacy, in speaking of one who has sacrificed so much in becoming the partner of an Indian missionary. I will simply add, that Mr. and Mrs. Howell, and their daughters Caroline and Elizabeth, were then, and are now, members of the Methodist Church.

In the spring which preceded my marriage, I was appointed by my people at Rice Lake, to transact some business for them at Toronto. I accordingly left Rice Lake and reached Toronto in April. Just before leaving for Rice Lake, I called to see my cousin, Thomas Kezhig, who was confined to his house by consumption. While on my journey homewards, between Toronto and Port Hope, as I was sleeping on one of the sofas of the steamboat, I had the following singular dream in relation to my cousin above mentioned:—

I found myself in a path on a wide plain, which led towards the south, between two cottages. I was impressed with a belief that it was my duty to proceed to the end of the road, which, from appearances, great multitudes had walked over. On nearing the cottages, I discovered a small gate, attended by a keeper. At first, he refused me an entrance, but after much persuasion, he permitted me to pass, extorting from me a promise, to return as soon as I should reach a certain spot, from which I could see the end of the path. I passed through the gate and traveled over a beautiful rolling country, with groves, flowers, and fruits, on my right and on my left, which delighted my eyes; while the singing of birds delighted my ears. I walked through several streams which ran smoothly over beds of beautiful pebbles. From one of these streams I drank, and felt much refreshed. In some places, I saw the impress of men's feet on the pebbles, which proved that persons had gone before me. Some time after this, I heard several voices conversing about the country to which they were traveling. I ascended a hill, from which I beheld a scene which no language can describe. In front was a large granite rock, in the form of a pyramid; it was exceedingly high; had seats on each side from the bottom to the top; and on these, sat a great multitude who had died in the Lord. Here and there was a vacant seat. Some, however, were standing, and all had a pair of wings. Those that were sitting, had wings, and seemed ready to fly! On the very summit, and above the rest, there was a spacious seat, or magnificent throne. One sat on this throne who shone like the sun! Over his crowned head was a circle, resembling a rainbow, on which was written, with letters of gold, "This is the King Jesus." What a splendid sight! it dazzled

GEORGE COPWAY

my eyes. Above his head were clouds of angels; these were performing beautiful gyrations. Sometimes they descended so low, that I could plainly see the upper side of their wings, which reflected a brilliant light from the throne. I did not hear them speak, but there was a noise like a mighty rushing wind, occasioned by their wings which were constantly in motion. There were myriads upon myriads of these winged angels; the very heavens were covered with them. I observed between me and this great rock, a river, part of which was as black as jet, and the rest as yellow as gold. It flowed gracefully along the edge of the beautiful green, near the rock. I saw two men plunge into its bosom, and swim. As soon as they reached the spot where the water was black, their clothes fell off of them, and were carried away by the current; while they themselves reached the shore on the opposite side. They now assumed forms too glorious for tongue or pen to describe; even imagination must fail here. They now seemed to rise up out of the river; and as they stood upon its bed, with their long white wings majestically expanded and dripping, they clapped their hands and exclaimed, "Glory to God in the highest; glory and honor to Jesus." They now stepped out of the stream, walked side by side, and ascended to the seats midway up the rock! While they were ascending, the entire multitude cheered and welcomed them. "Glory to God," "Halleluiah," with many other exclamations, were echoed in loud peals throughout the whole region. My eyes wept big burning tears, which overflowed my face. I tried to join the happy throng in exclamating *halleluiah;* and made several fruitless attempts to cross the river. I felt as if I were fettered, and fastened to a stake. Presently, I heard the sound of footsteps behind me; I turned around suddenly, and beheld my cousin Thomas Kezhig, passing along. I addressed him, and said, "Where are you going, cousin?" He replied, "I am going where my *mother* and *sister* have gone; but *you* must return home soon, for you are needed there; you will one day follow us to the skies." I exerted myself to approach him, but in vain. He turned about, ran down the hill to the water, plunged in, and swam like a duck. His clothes now fell off of him, as did those of the two individuals referred to above. I saw him rise; he exclaimed, "*Glory to Jesus!*" Some one exclaimed from the rock, "Thomas Kezhig is come, Thomas Kezhig is come." Immediately, two flew from their seats, and presented themselves before him, near the edge of the water. They embraced each other, and clapped their wings, as if filled with joy. O what a happy, happy scene! The immense throng of angelic beings witnessed this sight, and lowered their flight.

Those on the rock, now stood up at his approach, and flapped their wings. The two who had flown to him, led him by the hand to a seat. Every eye was now upon him; and the whole heavens seemed to echo, "*Welcome to thy rest, thou child of affliction.*" I recognized in these two, his mother and sister, who had died a few years before, with a hope full of glory. I could have given worlds for permission to cross the river. I wept sorely, and felt it incumbent to return, according to my promise, to the keeper of the gate. The keeper inquired, "well, did you see them?" But my heart was too full to give utterance to my thoughts. I now awoke, much agitated, and still weeping. I looked at my watch, and discovered that it was a quarter past one o'clock, P.M.

In the evening I met one of my step-brothers at Port Hope; he had just arrived. The first words that he uttered, were, "Our cousin is no more." I inquired, "When did he die?" He replied, "Today, about one o'clock." "Then," said I, "he is happy in the realms of bliss." The next day, as I stooped over his cold remains, I could still see his glorified spirit as in my dream, welcomed to the land of angels. O! "Let me, die the death of the righteous, and let my last end be like his." I loved him tenderly, and had good reason to believe that he also loved me. My readers will, I trust, excuse me for having inflicted upon them this dream. It is even now so vivid in my recollection, and being somewhat curious and peculiar, that I have ventured to give it. It is but a dream, and I wish it to go just for what it is worth, and no more.

I left Toronto for the west, on the third of June, and arrived at Buffalo the same evening, just in time to fulfil an engagement. I was to address the Sunday school Missionary Society at the Methodist Episcopal Church. I was obliged to leave Mrs. Copway at Toronto, as she was not quite prepared to depart; but the following day she met me in Buffalo. Here the brethren prevailed on us to stay over the Sabbath. Sabbath morning I preached at Black Rock, and in Buffalo in the evening. What a curious, inquisitive, and teasing people, some of the Yankees are! Yet, they are very friendly withal, for every one seemed to be striving to induce us to go to their homes to take tea and to pass the night. I had been married but a few days, and the following were some of the questions put to me:—"How did you obtain your wife?" "Where were you married?" "Did her father consent?" "How many of your people have married our white women?" These, and similar inquiries were constantly made, and were exceedingly annoying. But notwithstanding all this, I could say "farewell *dear friends* of Buffalo; thank you for your kindness, your good wishes, and your prayers. Farewell Sister Dobson, Brother M., and Brother Vanderpool"—a *noble* hearted and whole-souled man.

On the 7th of June, we parted with my wife's sister, Caroline, who had come with my wife from Toronto as far as Buffalo. We were soon sailing on Lake Erie. On the eighth we were in Cleveland. Here we were obliged to stop, as the regular boat for Detroit was engaged to convey persons to the great Whig Convention at Fort Meigs. But we passed a very agreeable time, however, especially with Mr. and Mrs. Peet. On the twelfth an opportunity offered by which we could go as far as Amherstburg, on our way to Detroit. The steamboat Milwaukie stopped at Cleveland on her route upwards, and on board of her we went. Soon we fell in with Rev. John Clark, who was on his way from the General Conference to Chicago, in company with Rev. Mr. Colclazier, of Detroit. It was my design to preach on board, but was prevented on account of the rolling of the boat, which caused much sea-sickness, and our early arrival at Amherstburg. Here we staid one week, and passed many happy hours, especially with Sister Scott. From Amherstburg we went to Detroit. On the eighteenth we started from Detroit for Mackinaw, on board the steamboat Robert Fulton, which place we reached on the twentieth; here we remained a few days with B. Chapman, Esq. Here I heard of the death of one of our traders, Lavaque, a pious man, and a particular friend. I preached his funeral sermon, and then his remains were consigned to the grave. Many wept on this occasion, for he was much beloved. Mrs. Copway was now suffering from chills and fever, which she first contracted at Toronto. On the twenty-third we took passage on board the steamboat Fairport, and arrived at Green Bay early the next morning. Mrs. Copway's indisposition induced me to remain here until she should feel better. Brother Chenoworth, the stationed preacher, was absent, and it devolved on me to fill his pulpit on the Sabbath. We had a most interesting season in waiting on the Lord. Mrs. Copway's fevers continued three weeks, and when it was thought that she had recovered, we took land carriage to Prairie Du Chien. But before we had gone many miles, she was again seized with chills and fever, and we were obliged to tarry at the house of a Mr. McCarty. His family were kind, and would not receive any compensation for their trouble. I now proposed to Mrs. C. to return to Green Bay, but she would not consent, saying, that as we had started, it were better to keep on. Every other day she had the fever. O how it distressed me to witness her affliction. We passed through the villages of the Stockbridge and

Brother-Town Indians. Their lands are good, and it is to be hoped that they will continue to conduct themselves well.

On the 17th of July we arrived at Winnebago Lake, where we took dinner with Brother White. After leaving this place, we had to kindle up a fire in the groves several times, in order to cook something for breakfast, and for the rest of the day; there being no settlers within twenty miles. Some men seem to have come to these "diggings" only for the purpose of defrauding travelers out of their goods and money. For every slim and dirty meal, we had to pay fifty cents. There is a house between Fort Winnebago and Prairie Du Chien which I can never forget. We had to pay fifty cents for each meal (?); twenty-five cents for lodging in beds swarming with fleas and bugs. Sleep was out of the question; so I spent the hours of the night on the seat of what was called a chair. August 23rd, we arrived at Prairie Du Chien, after much fatigue, having traveled ten days. Brother Kavanaugh had just arrived from St. Peters, and had us conveyed to Dubuque, in a canoe. Here, Mrs. Copway remained, till I returned from the Conference, which was held at Mount Morris. From Dubuque we went to Prairie Du Chien, in a steamboat; on the twenty-sixth we were compelled to go in our canoe to St. Peters, on account of the shallowness of the river. Our company consisted of Brothers Spates, Huddleston, Brown, Jones, Mrs. Copway, her sister, and myself. We encamped, occasionally, on the banks of the Mississippi. We were more than two weeks traveling three hundred miles, to St. Peters. We had a tent, which we pitched every night. On the 26th September, we had to mount the bluffs of the Mississippi River; here we found a number of Indian deities, made of stone. Mrs. Copway and her sister tumbled them all down into the river. Their worshippers must have been astounded and mortified when they returned, and discovered that their gods had vanished. On several occasions we were dripping wet. On the 9th of October we arrived at St. Peters; we here had the happiness and privilege of associating with the Presbyterian Missionaries three weeks; they were affectionate and truly kind to us. These, were Brothers Garvin, Pond, Denton, and their wives. We had yet to journey nearly three hundred miles. After some delay in getting ready, we started in our canoe. On the 27th of October we went about fifteen miles up the river; on the twenty-eighth we could proceed no farther on account of the ice. Now what was to be done? If the winter set in, while we are on our journey, we shall have to suffer much. We therefore concluded to go by land to Elk River Mission. On the twenty-ninth we hired a Frenchman to convey our things in his cart. It being late when we started, we walked but five miles the first day; we really dreaded the journey. On the thirtieth while we were crossing Rice River, the cart was upset; our provisions and clothes were filled with water; and many of our things were floating down the river. I made a fire, and we passed the rest of the day in drying our articles; fortunately, not one of us was in the cart. Mrs. Copway exhibited much patience and fortitude; she reproved us for murmuring, on account of this and other mishaps; and laughed, while our pies and cakes were sailing down the river. On the thirty-first we walked the whole day, and reached Rum River,—called so, because a barrel of rum had been concealed there. It would be too tedious to narrate *all* the circumstances connected with the rest of our journey.

On the 6th of November we arrived at the Mission, having traveled, in all, about two thousand and eighty miles. The Indians had fled from this Mission, on account of their enemies, the Sioux, whom they dreaded. Here, then, we had no employment; no one to instruct! We now endured much suffering. I was taken sick with the dysentery, and remained so four months, although, occasionally, I could move about. Brother Huddleston, also, became sick; he was taken on the 25th of December, and died on the thirtieth, of dysentery. This was truly a time of trial. We buried him near the banks of the Mississippi, on New Year's day. He had come here to do good; but O how inscrutable are the ways of God! The Chief of the Ojebwas had now arrived; and addressed us in the following language:—

"Brothers, I am sorry to see you all in such afflicting circumstances. I see that you loved him; and from what little I saw and knew of him, I believe he was a good man. He came here to do us good,—to teach our children. You ask me where you shall bury your Brother. I will tell you. Bury him on that little hill (pointing to it), so that we may see his grave as we pass up and down the river. I will tell my people to keep the grave in good order, and to respect it. No grass shall be allowed to grow too near it; we will see that it is weeded. Next summer, *I* will build a heap of stones about it, that all may see and know where the good man lies—he, who came to bless us. Tell his father, that the Sioux, our enemies, will not molest his remains."

This chief was not a pious man. Three of his warriors, now went to the hill, cleared away the snow, and dug the grave according to our directions. We committed his lifeless body to the cold grave in a strange land! I never knew how much I loved him, until he was gone. Filled with tears, sobs, and sighs, Brother Spates performed the last sad office, over the remains of our dearly beloved brother, while the rude blast was blowing the snow in every direction. Just before he died, he admonished and entreated us to meet him in heaven, where, he assured us, he was going. "Blessed are the dead, that die in the Lord."

The chief now invited us to go and reside with him at Rabbit River; and in February, we did so, after having traveled three days. During these three days, however, we had often to shovel away the snow, build a fire, and spread the bedding without any tent over it. We awoke one morning, and found the snow two inches deep on the bed clothes. We built a large fire, by which we warmed ourselves and boiled some coffee. Our bread was frozen; but we thawed it, and made a meal. When this was over, off we started. By the way, I ought to have mentioned that I had a poney for Mrs. Copway and her sister, on which they could ride. Through the winter he lived on rushes, and browsed like a deer. The poor fellow had to give out, about two miles before we reached Rabbit River; Mrs. Copway, therefore, had to walk this distance on the ice, which greatly fatigued her. On Saturday night quite late, we arrived at the shanty of Chief Hole-in-the-sky. In all our journeyings Mrs. C. was always ready and willing to endure every hardship. She never murmured nor appeared discontented. This, often encouraged me, and afforded us much relief. I record with gratitude, that God enabled her and her sister to bear up under the severest trials and hardships. We could have no earthly gain in view; the grace of God alone, therefore, supported us by day and by night, in sickness, in perils, in storms, in fatigues, in despondency, and in solitary places. At Rabbit River we labored with considerable success; but on account of the war raging between the Sioux and the Ojebwas, these two Missions, with that at Ottawa Lake, had to be abandoned.

Note A.

"1st. The soil at the Credit is generally very poor, and, consequently, the crops are light, and this, in a great measure, discourages our people from becoming good farmers. The situation of the Credit Reserve is better calculated for commercial than agricultural purposes.

"2nd. We have learned, by experience, that living together in a village, whilst endeavoring to follow farming, is attended with many disadvantages, and loss of time; it is therefore desirable, that all the Indians who wish to become planters, should be settled on their own lots.

"3rd. The evil example of many of the white people around our village, exposes our people to the temptation of drinking fire-water, and of committing other vices.

"4th. We are of opinion, that, if we go and settle on a good tract of land, many of our young men, who are now spending their time in idleness, would be induced to become industrious, and attend to their farming."

Note B.

GOVERNMENT HOUSE.
Kingston, 22nd July, 1841.

My Lord,

"I have the honor to acknowledge the receipt of your despatch of the 1st instant, No. 393, on the subject of the Indian Department in Canada. I beg to assure your Lordship that I have given the subject my attentive consideration, and I hope to be able to submit for your approval, a scheme for the consolidation of the Department. At the same time the matter is attended with great difficulty, arising from the peculiarity of the duties which the officers of the Department have to perform, the extent of country comprised within their jurisdiction, and, above all, from the system pursued with regard to the Indians, which, in my opinion, is of the most mistaken character. All my observation has completely satisfied me, that the direct interference of the Government is only advantageous to the Indians who can still follow their accustomed pursuits, and that if they became settlers, they should be compelled to fall into the ranks of the rest of Her Majesty's subjects, exercising the same Independent control over their own property and their own actions, and subject to the same general law as other citizens.

"The attempt to combine a system of pupilage with the settlement of these people in civilized parts of the country, leads only to embarrassment to the Government, expense to the Crown, a waste of the resources of the Province, and an injury to the Indians themselves. Thus circumstanced, the Indian loses all the good qualities of his wild state, and acquires nothing but the vices of civilization. He does not become a good settler, he does not become an agriculturist or a mechanic. He does become a drunkard and a debauchee, and his females and family follow the same course. He occupies valuable land, unprofitably to himself and injuriously to the country. He gives infinite trouble to the Government, and adds nothing either to the wealth, the industry, or the defence of the Province.

I have, &c.

(*Signed.*)   SYDENHAM

The Right Honorable
      Lord J. RUSSELL

XIV

I n the spring, we were out of provisions, and had to fish for a living for
about three weeks. Brother Spates taught school, and cousin Johnson
and myself visited the wigwams daily, for the purpose of singing and
praying, and reading the word of God. They always received us kindly;
and soon their minds and hearts began to feel serious, and they inclined
strongly towards Christianity. It was not long after that many of them
professed to have made their peace with God, and expressed their
determination to obey the precepts of Jesus. Here we must acknowledge
that God "made us glad according to the days wherein he has afflicted
us." We had "not labored in vain, nor spent our strength for nought,"
although we had to confess that we were unprofitable servants. While
conversing with a chief upon the importance of true religion, he became
much troubled, and admitted that his own religion was not as good as
the religion of the Bible; but, said he, "I will embrace your religion
when I shall have returned from one more battle with the Sioux; and I
will then advise my people to embrace it too." What a struggle this poor
fellow had within! His name was *Bah-goo-na-ge-shig* (Hole in the sky).
He had always been kind to me and mine; in the spring he presented to
me about eighty pounds of sugar; observing at the same time, "I have
brought this from the Sugar Bush today; you will require some for your
family; and I cheerfully give it."

Brother Brace and his family now arrived from Prairie Du Chien.
What tales of sufferings did they communicate! They had traveled six
hundred miles in the midst of winter; and were exposed to all winds and
weathers! But thank God now they were with us. Their clothes were
almost in strings, and their children were in rags! Expecting to find
enough to live on as soon as they arrived, they brought nothing with
them. Thank heaven we were just enabled to keep them and ourselves
from starving.

The Indians desired us to visit several other places, and establish
ourselves there. The whole country seemed ripe for the Gospel. It
was thought best that Brother Spates and myself should go down to
St. Peters, by water, and obtain provision. We were four days going,
and on our arrival, a war party was just on the eve of departing for our
Mission, where they intended to murder all the Ojebwas they could
find. I requested Brother Spates to accompany me back by land, to

inform the Indians of the intention of the Sioux. He said "there would be too much risk in going before the War Party." But my wife and sister were there; they, as well as my poor people, might be barbarously murdered. After repeated efforts to get some one to accompany me, but without success, I was determined to go alone. I trusted in the God of battles, and with his aid, I was confident that I could prevent these merciless and blood-thirsty warriors from imbruing their hands in the blood of my nation. I was ready for a start; and went to Chief Little-Crow's village, to tell him that I was going to the Rabbit River Mission. Not thinking that I was in earnest, or had courage enough, he said, "Tell Hole-in-the-sky, I am coming to get his scalp." This took place three hours before they were ready to march. In the midst of *jeers* and *war whoops*, I left their Mission house. They did not believe that I intended to go farther than Fort Snelling. As soon as I was out of sight, I began to run as fast as I was able. I called at the Post Office, which was nine miles from the Crow Mission, got my papers and letters, and ran about seven miles over the Prairie, without stopping. I bought a pony on the road, of a Frenchman, and having no saddle, I rode but three miles of the whole distance. I tied my pack on his back, and made him run all the afternoon. In the night I slept without a fire. I was so anxious to get home, that I had no appetite for eating, the first two days. I went at the rate of about seventy-five miles per day, and arrived home at noon, on the fourth day; having walked two hundred and forty miles, forded eight large streams, and crossed the broad Mississippi twice. My coat and pantaloons were in strips. I crossed the Mississippi just in front of our Mission house, and as soon as possible, I told the chief that the war party were now on their way to our Mission, to kill them. I advised him to lead away the women and children, which they did, and the next day they *all* left us. We, that is, my family, myself, and the other missionaries, were now left to the mercy of the Sioux. But they did not come, although they sent spies. Brother Brace, Cousin Johnson, and I, now ventured to take our families down to St. Peters. We left in a large bark canoe, and had only *one loaf* of bread, *two quarts* of beans, and *two quarts* of molasses. Brother Brace was so sick, that we had to lift him in and out of the canoe.

We saw tracks of the war party, on our way to St. Peters. They watched us on the river, as we heard afterwards. We encamped about one mile and a half this side of their watching place, during the night, and did not know that they knew this fact, as will be seen in the sequel. They came and held a council just across the river from our encampment; they could see the light of our fire. The war chiefs agreed that four of the warriors should swim over to us and take us all prisoners. One was to take the canoe to the other side of the river, to bring over the rest of the party. They were to kill me, and my Cousin Johnson. But the chief said to them, "If you kill these men, the Great Spirit will be angry, and he will send his white children to kill us, and our children."

One of the warriors told the chief that he was a coward, and that he ought to have remained at home. To this, the chief replied, "I am no coward; and we will see who are cowards when we come in front of our enemies." Thus they disputed, and even quarrelled, among themselves, till day-light. The same morning, we left without breakfast, and on the morning following, we were beyond their reach.

We saw where they had raised a number of logs, so that they might lie in ambush. I ought to mention, that we were perfectly ignorant of all their plans and actions, until we arrived at St. Peters. The chief, himself, communicated to us what has been stated above, in the presence of his warriors.

This country, is, indeed, a dangerous place for the Ojebwa Missionaries; but not so for the whites, for they never pretend to interfere with them, in any way.

Before Conference, and while I was obliged to be at their mission, for there was no other road for us to go, the Sioux tried to intimidate me by pointing their guns to my breast, and by flourishing their war clubs about my head; they would say, "I wish you had *longer hair*, so that I could take a good hold of it and scalp you." I cannot describe my *feelings*, on this occasion, better, than by quoting, with a little alteration, from the immortal bard of Avon:—"they were so terrible, that they shook my soul, and made my seated heart knock at my ribs against the use of nature; cold drops of sweat hung on my trembling flesh, my blood grew chilly, and I seemed to freeze with horror." I would often go and see them in their Tepees (wig-wams); this was good policy. They frequently showed me some of the scalps of the Ojebwas, and danced the scalping dance. What awful noises they made, as they danced in their fantastic dresses, with their faces painted black. They reminded me much of his Satanic and fiendish majesty, rejoicing over a damned spirit entering hell.

During this summer, I accompanied Brother Kavanaugh to Sandy Lake Mission, at the head of the Mississippi. I returned by the Falls of St. Anthony, while Brother Kavanaugh went by the way of Lake Superior, he having business with the American Fur Company. When I arrived, I learned that the elder son of Brother Kavanaugh had been drowned; he fell from a ledge of rocks. Sister Kavanaugh felt deeply, this mercifully severe dispensation. Brother Kavanaugh now arrived; poor man! he could not speak to me for some time. I met him some distance from his house; he had heard of the circumstance, but had not, as yet, been home. "How unsearchable are God's judgments; and his ways past finding out." Yet, withal, in such dark hours, many a christian sees parental Love. Ah! we may often exclaim, in the language of good old Jacob, "All these things are against me," but we may also say, God orders every thing for the good of his own.

That summer we went to Conference, which was held in Platteville. I was then appointed to establish a Mission at Fon du Lac, at the head of Lake Superior. Brother James Simpson was appointed school teacher.

We traveled from the Sioux Mission up the St. Croix River, crossed over to Burnt-wood River, and thence to Lake Superior. Having provided food, I departed with Mrs. Copway and her sister, John Jacob, Massey, and Brother Simpson, about the fifteenth of September. We were two weeks on the St. Croix River; and part of this time I was so sick as to become delirious. I was just able to walk over the two mile portage to Burnt-wood River. The other men, therefore, had to carry the large canoe the two miles; this was hard, but it was impossible for me to help them. We were now out of provisions. I have been told, by good authority, the following singular fact. There is but one spring which forms the two rivers;—the St. Croix which runs down to the Mississippi, and the Burnt-wood River which runs down to Lake Superior.

In going down the Burnt-wood River, our progress was slow. We were out of provisions from Thursday, till Sabbath morning, when we arrived at Fon du Lac. On Saturday, Mrs. Copway and her sister had a small piece of bread between them; the rest lived upon *hope*. In the afternoon, we rowed about twenty-eight miles, and on Sabbath morning just at day-break we had to start for our station, Fon du Lac; about twelve o'clock we arrived there, and saw John Lawndree, the trader, who was celebrated for his hospitality. I shook hands with him; he asked me if I were sick; and said, "You look pale." I told him, we were all hungry, and had had nothing to eat but a small piece of bread since Friday evening. "Ah, indeed!" said he, "I will soon have breakfast for you." Mrs. Laundree, after a few minutes, had every thing necessary for our cheer and comfort. While eating, I thought, that whatever might be said of Catholics, this was truly a Christian act; and heaven will not let it pass unnoticed.

In the evening I addressed a company of traders and Indians. I found the Indians in a miserable state; the cause of which, I attribute wholly to their intercourse with the traders, the principal part of whom are notoriously wicked and profane. I felt very thankful, however, that we were here; yet I was filled with anxieties; for how should I begin my labors? Brother Simpson and I, commenced by fitting up the old mission house, formerly occupied by the Rev. Mr. Ely, who had taught many to read and write. The school house, also, was fitted up, and in it Brother Simpson taught, till the spring. Our prospects seemed to brighten up, and we had good reason to think that the Indians were glad to have us with them; for they sent their children regularly to school, and our religious meetings were well attended. During the winter several became seriously and religiously affected; and in the spring, a few believed that they had experienced a change of heart. This encouraged us much. I can never forget the happy seasons I enjoyed, in my visits from house to house, and in the woods. I endeavored to seek out all; and the good Master was gracious to me. I have often traveled about among them on snow shoes, weeping for joy. Often too, did I sleep alone in the woods, having had to dig away the snow to prepare a place to lie on. Though frequently hungry, faint, and lonely, I enjoyed the presence of the Lord, On one occasion I was sorely tried:—I accompanied one of the traders about one hundred and eighty miles, to purchase cattle for our place. I bought a cow for my own immediate family; and in the spring, it was killed and eaten by the Indians. Had they been in want, there might have been some excuse for such an act. We expected her to "come in" in about three weeks, and her milk was to be our chief dependence. It was a cruel piece of work. After having traveled too, three hundred and sixty miles for the express purpose of obtaining her, and then to be thus deprived, was a hard case truly. Had she lived, many of the children of the Indians would have shared in the milk. When will the poor Indians be instructed in right principles?

From a long experience, and close observations among the Sioux and the Ojebwas, in regard to the hostile feelings existing between them, I have been brought to the following conclusions:

1. That Christianity and education alone, will check their malevolent and hostile feelings, and thus put an end to their bloody wars. For this end, missionaries must be sent to both nations.
2. That it is useless to send missionaries without suitable interpreters to assist them.
3. That Missions should be established in the vicinities of the borders of the neutral grounds of these two powerful and savage nations; because in these places there is but little, if anything, to excite them to revenge.
4. That wherever a Mission is once established, it must never be abandoned.
5. That where any Protestant Mission is established in any village, no other denomination should establish another in the same place, or interfere in any other way.
6. That missionaries ought to assist each other whenever they happen to fall in each other's way, or are requested to do so.
7. That missionaries ought not to preach their own peculiar doctrines, to the disadvantage of other denominations; for this not only lessens their own influence, but likewise that of others.

The scenery near the head of Lake Superior, is almost as splendid as that of the beautiful Hudson. There is a magnificent fall about eight miles above the Mission. The Indians often kill moose, bears, and deer, in this region. In the spring, summer, and fall, they live on fish. As we had no salt, we were obliged to preserve our fish by hanging them on poles, with their heads downwards, and in this manner they would freeze. When the spring arrived, they began to thaw, and becoming soft, would fall from the poles. Late in the fall, white fish ascend the rapids, and can be scooped up with nets. In the spring, fish of every kind, and in great abundance, ascend these rapids.

On the 9th of April, 1842, it pleased the Lord to bless us with a son. This was our first child—a fine healthy boy. We thanked God for his goodness and mercy in preserving all our lives in the desert, and while surrounded by savages. I committed and commended him to God. May he live to take his station in the missionary field.

Brother Kavanaugh was kind enough to visit us; he returned by the way of Sandy Lake Mission. I accompanied him over the first

Portage; here we knelt down on the green, and worshipped the God of Missions. We now parted; but I still hope to see this affectionate brother again, even in this world. But if we shall never meet on earth, I trust, we shall, in heaven, "where the wicked cease from troubling, and the weary are at rest."

> *"Where we shall forget our sorrows and pains,*
> *And with our Redeemer in glory shall reign,*
> *Shall sing the anthems resouuding on high,*
> *And bathe in the ocean that never shall dry."*

XV

We were often delightfully associated with the Presbyterian Missionaries at La Pointe, the Rev. Messrs. Hall and Wheeler, and their amiable families. Their benevolence and christian courtesy are above any praise that we can render; but we would acknowledge that our hearts overflow with great gratitude whenever we recall them to mind. It was here that I became acquainted with the Rev. Mr. Boutwell. I preached for these beloved brethren several times, and we enjoyed sweet communion, and some thrilling seasons together.

The Council of the Ojebwa nation assembled in this place about the first of October. The government agent, R. Stewart, of Detroit, treated with them for their mineral regions, for which the Government gave them a large amount in money. From this time, I shall date the dissipation, misery, and ruin, of this part of our nation.

1. Because it induces speculators to visit them yearly to sell their goods at enormous prices; and their whiskey, which inevitably ruins both body and soul.
2. Because it opens the door for all sorts of unprincipled men and vagabonds. The miners, too, many of whom, are no better than pickpockets.
3. Because, in possessing so much money without any correct views of economy, utility, or prudence, it becomes to them "the root of all evil"—a curse instead of a blessing.

In these appropriations, the American Government have grossly erred. What benefit can the many thousands of dollars, which are paid annually, be to the Indians, if they are not capable of exercising any judgment in relation to a proper use of money? The fact is, that, at the end of every year, they are sunk into deeper degradation. I would now ask, what are millions of money without education? I do not mean that an *equivalent* should not be given for lands ceded to the Government. No; but I do mean that this equivalent should be appropriated in such a way as to produce the greatest benefits and the happiest results. If a certain amount had been given in cash, another amount in cattle and farmer's utensils, another in clothing, another in houses and school houses, and the like; and with these, if a few mechanics, farmers, and teachers, had been sent among them, the Indians might have become industrious, intelligent, and useful citizens. One third of each annual payment would be sufficient to educate, and to supply all the wants of, their children. It may be supposed by some, that the white people, settled near them, give them good advice, and urge upon them the propriety and necessity of appropriating their monies in the manner just suggested. Yet this is not only *not the case*, but these very whites, at least a large majority of them, are continually laying plans by which they can extort from these unlettered and ignorant Indians, whatever they possess. I write not at random, on these matters. I am too well acquainted with them from painful observation and bitter experience. I have been present at *ten* payments; viz. at Sault St. Marie, Mackinaw, Green Bay, Prairie Du Chien, and St. Peters. During these payments, quantities of whiskey were brought to the Indians, or else, they were seduced to go elsewhere to purchase it. Poor untutored red men! you were deluded, and made drunk by white men, and then in your hellish and drunken passions, you turned around, and imbrued your hands in the blood of your own relatives, and brethren. And were I to narrate some of the scenes which occurred among the white faces (with black hearts), on these occasions, it would sicken the heart; nay, it would make mad the guilty, and appal the innocent. The very devil himself might shudder.

It was now two years since I left Canada; I received letters from there, from the Rev. Messrs. Stinson, Green, and Jones, requesting me to return home and labor with them. At first, I did not deem it advisable to go, because I felt under many obligations to those who had sent me to school for two years; and had rendered me other kind services. But it was not until after repeated solicitations had been made, and money to defray my traveling expenses had been remitted, that I consented. I obtained permission from my Superintendent, Rev. J. R. Goodrich, to depart. I left La Pointe, Oct. 10th, in the schooner Algonquin for Sault St. Marie. From there we took a row boat for Mackinaw, and at M. took a steamboat for Buffalo; we now proceeded onwards and arrived at Toronto on the 28th of October. My wife's parents, and relatives, and very many dear friends were delighted to see us again, after an absence of two years. We found them all well, and felt grateful to God for another expression of his abundant goodness and mercy. I spent much of my time in narrating the scenes we had witnessed, and a full account of my mission.

In about a month, I was sent to Credit river, (Mrs. C. remained behind in her father's family). Here I taught school till Christmas, when I began traveling with Rev. Wm. Ryerson, on a Missionary tour towards Montreal. We were absent about three months, and preached or spoke every day. We collected about a thousand dollars per month. The eloquence and piety of brother R. seemed to be duly appreciated wherever we went. He is the best platform speaker, that I have ever heard in the Methodist connexion. I had supposed, however, that he would be dull and monotonous; but this was far, very far from the fact.

Having returned from this tour, to Toronto, I was next appointed by the Missionary Society to labor at the Saugeeng Mission, in the place of the Rev. Thomas Williams. On this journey my wife accompanied me. The distance was one hundred and sixty miles; and we reached there on the 12th of April, '43. On our way, we stopped at Goderich; and from thence we took a canoe about sixty-five miles.

I entered upon my duties as a missionary among the Christian Indians. I met with difficulties, for I could obtain nothing without money; and even when a request was made, it was not met by the Society. I could not be convinced that it was my duty to starve, and therefore concluded I must leave. My Indian brethren stepped forward at this time, and petitioned Governor Metcalf, to afford me a living from the Government. Their request was granted, and I was paid by Government $400 per year, for three years. I should have continued here, but the next year my services were demanded among my relatives at Rice Lake.

In the summer, I took Mrs. Copway to Toronto, and left her at her father's, while I was absent at Montreal with the Rev. Mr. Jones. Here, we waited on the the Governor General, and presented our views, and those of our people, respecting the formation of a Manual Labor School for the benefit of the Indians. The Governor expressed himself as favorably disposed, but was too sick to take an active part in it. But before this, the Canada Conference had appointed Rev. P. Jones and myself, to visit the Missions, and ascertain how much each Mission was willing to contribute for this object.* During this fall, Mr. Jones and family left for England.

I returned to Toronto and took my family back to Saugeeng Mission. While on our passage, in a schooner, our little son, who was about

---

* The amount reported from the Indians alone, was $2,800.

three years old, fell overboard; we heard him fall into the water. I ran immediately to the side of the vessel and jumped into the lake. The schooner was sailing quite rapidly, and had passed him about twenty yards. I swam as fast as possible, and saw him sink. When I reached the spot where he sank, I dove down about seven feet, seized hold of him, and brought him to the surface. As the waves were running high, it was with the greatest difficulty that that I could keep him above the water so that he could breathe; and I was compelled at times to let him sink an instant, that I might breathe myself. I heard him cry, which was encouraging, for I was fearful that he was dying. At one time I almost despaired of saving either of our lives. I was about giving up all hope, when I saw the yawl boat near me, and I was told that I was just about sinking, when the captain rescued us from a watery grave. The captain, and all on board, were so frightened, that they lost some time in concluding what to do. Had they luffed at once, and despatched the yawl, two or three minutes might have been saved. But, I ought not to complain; our lives were spared, and thanks be to a kind Providence for his timely deliverance. I then gave him up to God, and prayed that he might be preserved, and be devoted to the cause of Christ.

We now resumed our labors at the Mission. While at this station there were many hopeful conversions. A remarkable circumstance is, that during the whole three years of my sojourn in this field of labor, I never knew but *one single case* in which fire-water was used. I must not omit noticing here, a very faithful teacher in my charge, Jacob Jackson; his influence was of the best kind; he was also a very pleasant and interesting singer. It had been but a few years since these Indians were converted. They now have good farms, dwellings, school houses, meeting houses, and a saw mill. How wonderful are the effects of the gospel! They also take delight in praying, and in singing the praises of God. Had the American Government adopted the same course towards the La Pointe Indians, that the British Government adopted towards these, the same lasting blessings would have ensued.

XVI

Of late, the General Councils of the christianized Ojebwas have been convened, and conducted, in the same manner as public and other business meetings are conducted among the whites. The last General Council, which consisted of Ojebwas and Ottawas, was held at Saugeeng. The chiefs came from Lakes St. Clair, Huron, Ontario, and Simcoe, and from Rice and Mud Lakes. The object of this convention was to devise plans by which the tract of land now owned by the Saugeeng Indians, could be held for the sole benefit of the Ojebwa Nation; to petition the Government for aid in establishing a Manual Labor School; to ascertain the views and feelings of the chiefs in relation to forming one large settlement among themselves at Owen's Sound, there to live in future; and to attend to other things of minor importance. There were forty-eight chiefs present, from Canada West alone. Chief Sawyer took the chair, and the writer had the honor of being Vice-President. Chief John Jones, of Owen Sound, was selected to deliver the opening address, in which he was to give an outline of the subjects to be discussed. The meeting was now called to order; and after singing, and an appropriate prayer by Chief John Sunday, Chief Jones arose; all was silent, and every eye was turned towards him. After rolling his small but piercing black eye over the vast assembly, he spoke as follows:—

"Brothers! You have been called from all parts of Canada, and even from the north of Georgian Bay. You are from your homes, your wives, and your children. We might regret this, were it not for the circumstances that require you here.

"Fellow Chiefs, and Brothers, I have pondered with deep solicitude, our present condition; and the future welfare of our children, as well as of ourselves. I have studied deeply and anxiously, in order to arrive at a true knowledge of the proper course to be pursued to secure to us and to our descendants, and even to others around us, the greatest amount of peace, health, happiness, and usefulness. The interests of the Ojebwas and the Ottawas are near and dear to my heart; for them, I have passed many sleepless nights, and have often suffered from an agitated mind. These nations, I am proud to say, are my brothers; many of them, are bone of my bone, and for them, if needs be, I could willingly, nay, cheerfully, sacrifice any thing. Brothers, you see my heart. (Here, the speaker held out a piece of *white paper*, emblematical of a *pure* heart.)

GEORGE COPWAY

"Fellow Chiefs and Warriors! I have looked over your wigwams throughout Canada, and have arrived at the conclusion, that you are in a warm place; your neighbors, the whites, are kindling fires all around you (that is, clearing the lands). One purpose for which you have been called together, is to devise some plan by which we can live together, and become a happy people, so that our dying fires may not go out (our nation may not become extinct), but may be kindled in one place, which will prove a blessing to our children.

"Brothers! Some of you are living on small parcels of land, and others, on Islands, We now offer you any portion of the land which we own in this region; that we may, the rest of our days, smoke the pipe of friendship; live and die together; and see our children play, and be reared on one spot. We ask no money of you. We love you; and because we love you, and feel for your children, we propose this.

"Brothers! There are many other subjects which we think ought to come under your consideration, besides those already stated. But the most important are:

"1. Whether it would not be better for the whole Ojebwa Nation to reside on this, our territory.
"2. Would it not be well to devise ways and means to establish Manual Labor Schools for the benefit of the nation.
"3. Ought not a petition be drawn up and presented to our Great Father (the Governor General), for the purpose of fixing upon a definite time for the distribution of the annual "presents," and the small annuities of each tribe.
"4. Is it not desirable to petition the Governor General, to appoint a resident Indian interpreter, to assist the agent in Toronto.
"5. As we (the Christian part of our nation) have abandoned our former customs and ceremonies, ought we not to make our own laws, in order to give character and stability to our chiefs, as well as to empower them to treat with the Government under which we live, that they may, from time to time, present all our grievances and other matters to the General Government.

"My Chiefs, Brothers, Warriors! This morning, (the speaker now pointed his finger towards heaven) look up, and see the blue sky; there are no clouds; the sun is bright and clear. Our fathers taught us, that at such assemblies when the sky was without clouds, the Great Spirit was smiling upon them. May he now preside over us, that we may make a long, smooth, and straight path for our children. It is true, I seldom see you all; but this morning, I shake hands with you all in my heart.

"Brothers! This is all I have to say."

On taking his seat eighty-four Chiefs responded, "*Hah!*" an exclamation of great applause.

Several chiefs spoke, and highly approved of what had been proposed; and expressed their gratitude for the kind offer of the lands. It was proposed to petition his Excellency the Governor, to grant and secure to the Indians, the whole of this territory.

The following was drawn up by John Jones, Jacob Jackson, and David Wa-wa-nosh.

The Petition of the Ojebwa Chiefs, in General Council, respecting the unceded lands north of Saugeeng and Owen's Sound. June 5th, 1845.

To our Great Father Lord METCALF, Governor General of British North America, and Captain General of the same, &c., &c.

The OJEBWA CHIEFS in General Council assembled, HUMBLY SHEWETH:

FATHER—Your Petitioners having ceded a great portion of their once extensive territory about Saugeeng and Owen's Sound, and a portion of it having been restored to them since the treaty of 1836, by your Excellency's gracious commands;

FATHER—Your Petitioners are very anxious that the Reserve (now still known as the Indian Territory), be a perpetual reserve, as a future refuge for a general colonization of the Ojebwa Nation, comprising the scattered Tribes in Canada West;

FATHER—And that these lands may now and forever be opened to all the Tribes; that whenever any Tribe is disposed to move, that they may have nothing to fear, but have access to any of the good lands to settle upon;

Father—You have settled your white children on those lands that once were our father's; we ask now to let us have the only remaining land we have, to ourselves, unmolested;

Father—This is the prayer of your red children; and feeling confident that you will give it every important consideration which it requires, your red children will listen to hear the answer of their Great Father. And they, as in duty bound, will ever pray.

Forty-seven names, besides that of the President, were attached to this petition.

Never was I more delighted than with the appearance of this body. As I sat and looked at them, I contrasted their former (degraded), with their present (elevated) condition. The Gospel, I thought, had done all this. If any one had told me twenty years ago, that such would be their condition, I should have ridiculed the idea, and set the narrator down for a fool or a maniac. This assembly was not convened for the purpose of devising schemes of murder; plans by which they could kill their enemies; but to adopt measures by which peace, harmony, and love, might be secured, and a "smooth and straight path" made for their children. I see nothing at present, to hinder them from increasing in knowledge, happiness, and usefulness, except the conduct of the Government Agents, many of whom are inimical to our nation, and often prove a curse to her.

Several other papers were drawn up, and signed by the President, by order of the General Council. One of these I must be allowed to give, although it concerns myself.

To all to whom it may concern. In the General Council of the Ojebwa nation of Indians. We, the Chiefs, of the various Tribes of the Ojebwa Indians, do hereby appoint, and authorize our beloved brother, the Rev. George Copway, as our agent for the Manual Labor School, to procure subscriptions for the same, believing that this will be one of the greatest means, if established, of raising our young men, to become like our

White brothers; to learn industry, economy, and to gain knowledge, that we may become a happy and a prosperous people.

    Signed by order of the General Council.

JOSEPH SAWYER, (L. S.)

President of the General Council of the Ojebwa Nation.
Saugeeng, July 4, 1845.

I will also give an extract of my letter to the Rev. Mr. Wilkinson, who was then President of the Canada Conference, immediately after the close of the General Council.

(Extract from Letter Book, Page 151.)

SAUGEENG MISSION,}
July 14, 1845 }

To the President of the Conference, Rev. MR. WILKINSON.

*   *   *   *   *   *   *

The late General Council, have appointed me their agent for the Manual Labor School. I shall be happy to receive any instructions you may think proper to give, on my way down (to Montreal), for I am anxious to see this going on.

*   *   *   *   *   *   *

I remain Yours, &c.,

GEORGE COPWAY,
Missionary at Saugeeng.

I give these, for the benefit and instruction of those, who have been so kind as to insinuate, or assert, that I was not an *authorized agent* to forward the interests of my poor people. Those who have been the loudest and most active in this slander, have done the least, in rendering the Indians any essential service. Let them go on, with their gossipings, while I go on my way rejoicing in doing all I can for my poor people, independently of the Canada Conference. Neither have I any disposition to court the favor of this Conference. Indeed, my heart has often sickened, at the divisions and subdivisions of the Canada Methodists.

The speeches of Jones, Sunday, Taunchey, McCue, D. Sawyer, J. Youngs, W. Herkermer, were excellent. That of John Sunday, particularly, was uncommonly eloquent. His keen black eyes, flashing fire; and his large brawny arms extended, gave great effect to his speech. As a matter of course, there were often differences of opinion, as well as warm discussions, upon various subjects; some would even feel that their views were not fairly treated; still, there were no unkind remarks, no calling of hard names, no abuse, no ridicule, no insults, no threats, no intrigues, no blows, and *no challenges to meet on the field of* HONOR (?). The individual who had the floor, was never interrupted; profound attention was given, and a death-like silence was observed. Occasionally, it is true, there was perpetrated a pleasant, and innocent *jeu d' esprit;* an example of which, I will give.

During a protracted debate, in which Chief John Jones took a very active part, some facts were elicited, and some views were presented, which induced him to change some of his former opinions, and vote on the other side. One of the speakers at the close of his remarks, referred to this fact, and observed, very good humoredly, "If he wishes to be like a *fish worm without a head*— capable of moving forwards or backwards, let him alone."

I have often been asked the question, "What is the reason that the Indians are diminishing in numbers in the midst of their white neighbors?" To state all that might be said in replying to this question, would require almost a separate volume. But the following are a few of the principal reasons:—

1. The introduction of King Alcohol among them.
2. The introduction of new diseases, produced by their intercourse with the whites; and by adopting their intemperate habits.
3. Their inability to pursue that course of living, after abandoning their wigwams, which tends to health and old age.
4. Their spirits are broken down in consequence of seeing that their *race* are becoming homeless, friendless, moneyless, and trodden down by the whites.
5. Their future prospects are gloomy and cheerless—enough to break down the noblest spirits.

There are many other reasons which could be assigned for their diminution. But are not these sufficient of themselves to crush and exterminate even any *white* race, if not protected and defended by friends and wholesome laws? Our people have been driven from their homes, and have been cajoled out of the few sacred spots where the bones of their ancestors and children lie; and where they themselves expected to lie, when released from the trials and troubles of life. Were it possible to reverse the order of things, by placing the whites in the same condition, how long would it be endured? There is not a white man, who deserves the name of *man*, that would not rather die, than be deprived of his home, and driven from the graves of his relatives. "Oh shame, where is thy blush!"

With all the wholesome and enlightened laws; with all the advantages and privileges of the glorious Gospel, that shines so richly and brightly all around the white man; the poor ignorant Indians are compelled, at the point of the bayonet, to forsake the sepulchres of those most dear to them, and to retire to a strange land, where there is no inhabitant to welcome them!!! May the day soon dawn, when Justice will take her seat upon the throne.

If I did not think that there were some who are alive to the interests of my people, and often shed a tear for them; if I did not think that I could discover a gleam of light and hope in the future, "I should of all men be most miserable;" "Surely the bitterness of death" would be "past." I look then to the Gospel and to education as my only hope.

I will now state, in a very brief manner, what I think ought to be done, by those whose benevolent feelings lead them to commiserate the condition of the Aborigines of America.

1. They should establish missions and high schools wherever the whites have frequent intercourse with them.
2. They should use their influence, as soon as the Indians are well educated, and understand the laws of the land, to have them placed on the same footing as the whites.
3. They should try to procure for them a territorial or district government, so that they may represent their own nation.
4. They should obtain for them, deeds of their own lands; and, if qualified, according to law, urge their right to vote.

The Indians will be sure to waste and squander whatever they may receive from the American or British Governments, unless *some*, at least, of the above suggestions, shall have been put into practice.

The Council was now dissolved. The President, Chief Sawyer, proceeded to His Excellency, the Governor General, and presented the petitions, in the name of the General Council. These petitions, as we learned afterwards, were received with a simple *nod!* of the head. O mercy! is this forever to be our destiny? Common humanity at least, might have induced his Lordship to speak a few consolatory words, if nothing else. Our reception was both discouraging and chilling. When we have a Press of our own, we shall, perhaps, be able to plead our own cause. Give us but the *Bible*, and the influence of a *Press*, and we ask no more.

The General Council appointed me to go to Walpole, to present their address to the Walpole Island Indians, entreating them to embrace Christianity. I visited them in July.

XVII

A Geographical Sketch of the Ojebwa, Or Chippeway, Nation

As the Ojebwa Nation are within the bounds of the two governments—the American and the British, I will give a separate account of each. The number of our nation, according to Drake, in 1842, was thirty thousand; and this is not far from the truth. The best work upon the Indians, however, is that deservedly popular book, by Col. McKinney, of New-York; the *undoubted* friend of the red man.

I will now speak of that part of the nation who occupy places within the bounds of the United States. They inhabit all the northern part of Michigan, or the south shore of Lake Huron; the whole northern part of Wisconsin Territory; all the south shore of Lake Superior, for eight hundred miles; the upper part of the Mississippi, and Sandy, Leach, and Red Lakes.

That part of our nation who live in the British possessions, occupy from Gononaque, below Kingston, throughout all western Canada; the north of Lake Huron; the north of Lake Superior; the north of Lake Winepig; the north of Red River Lake, about one hundred miles. The whole extent, therefore, occupied is over one thousand nine hundred miles east and west, and from two to three hundred miles north and south.

There are over five thousand living under the British Government, and less than twenty-five thousand under the American Government. There are about five thousand of these who receive religious instructions; missionaries of different denominations being sent from Canada and the United States. The Methodists were the first who preached to the Ojebwas, or Massissaugas (as they are frequently called). They commenced at Credit River, in Canada West, in 1824, and at Grape island, in 1827. The conversion of some of the Ojebwas commenced during those years. Native teachers were then sent to their brethren in the West, where the influence of Christianity is still felt. There are twenty-three Methodist Missionary Stations; six of which, are in the States, and the remainder in Canada. There are four Presbyterian Missions, all of which are in the States; viz. La Pointe, Bad River, Leach Lake, and Red Lake. There are seven Episcopalian Mission Stations; all of which are in Canada, except one, which is at Green Bay. There are two Baptist Mission Stations, one at Sault St. Marie, and the other at Green Bay. The Roman Catholics have their missionaries in nearly all the principal places in the west.

Those who are not under religious instruction, although accessible, are wandering without the gospel. There is a field in the Territory of Wisconsin where missionaries should be sent. There are Indians all around the shores of Lake Superior who have, from time to time, called for missionaries, and have not yet been supplied. The Hudson's Bay Company have, of late, adopted a plan which in my opinion does them much credit; they employ missionaries to give instruction to the Indians and their children in the principles of Christianity. There are persons who once belonged to other nations, who now live in the territory of the Ojebwas.

The present state of the christianized Ojebwas is such, that they are fully ripe for greater advancement in religion, literature, and the arts and sciences. Multitudes have left their wigwams, their woods, and the chase, and are now endeavoring to tread in the footsteps of worthy white men. The reasons for all this, are the following:

1. Their chiefs have seen the necessity of making a "smooth, straight path for their children," by appropriating as much of their means as they could spare.
2. The rising generation are beginning to thirst for learning, and are cultivating a taste for improvement more than ever.
3. Native teachers are now being trained to go to their brethren, and preach to them in their own language, Christ, and him crucified. By this means the nation must be elevated.

Our prospects as a nation, are becoming brighter through missionary efforts. There are many in Wisconsin, and at Lake du Flambeau, who have requested that missionaries be sent along the south shore of Lake Superior. The same may be said of those residing about Winepeg and Red Lakes. Much of the western part of Red Lake, is full of "the habitations of cruelty;" for the Chippewas and Sioux are habitually destroying each other.

I will here give extracts from the Report of the Commissioners, in 1842, to the Provincial Parliament, relative to the Mission Stations; also subjoin the names of the villages with their condition, and the chiefs of each village, as far as I could ascertain them, which will show their progress, and their present state; and also those who have abandoned the wigwam and the chase, and resort to farming for a living.

1. Chippewas of the River Thames

The Chippewas and Munsees occupy a tract of land containing about 9000 acres, in the Township of Caradoc, within the London District, at a distance of about twenty-five miles from the Moravian village. It is only within ten years that the Chippewas have been reclaimed from a wandering life, and settled in their present location. The Munsees have been settled since the year 1800, on land belonging to the Chippewas, with the consent of that tribe. The present number of Chippewas is 378, and of Munsees 242.

The Chippewas and Munsees are not collected in a village, but live on small farms scattered over their tract. Some of the Chippewas are settled on surveyed lots of twenty acres each. This tribe occupies 76 log houses, and six wigwams; they possess 25 barns. They have 450 acres under cultivation. Their stock consists of 30 oxen, 27 cows, 44 heifers, 82 horses and colts, and 400 swine. Their agricultural implements include 9 ploughs, 9 harrows, 23 scythes and sickles, 19 ox chains, a fanning mill, 4 wagons and carts, 7 spades, &c.; they have a blacksmith's forge, and two and a half setts of carpenters' tools.

JOHN RILEY, *Chief*

2. The Chippewas at Amherstburg

They all profess christianity, and several of them are examples of true piety. The majority are Wesleyan Methodists, and the others Roman Catholics. They have no place of Worship of their own. They can command the means. The Methodist minister, however, who is stationed in the town of Amherstburg, visits those of his persuasion every Sunday, and with the aid of an Interpreter, preaches, reads and expounds the Scripture to them. They also have a general Prayer Meeting among themselves, once a fortnight, and they meet occasionally more privately for social prayer; some of them maintain family worship. The Roman Catholics attend chapel at Amherstburg, which is about three miles from their settlement.

There is at present no school among them, but they have expressed their desire to establish one, and would gladly avail themselves of instruction for their children. When there was one, the attendance of the scholars was very irregular, but their ability in acquiring knowledge was in no way inferior to that of the white children.

3. Chippewas of the St. Clair

These Indians are among the first whom Sir John Colborne endeavored to settle and civilize. Previously to 1830, they were wandering heathens like their brethren elsewhere, scattered over the western part of the Upper Province; they were drunken and dissipated in their habits, and without either religious or moral restraint. In 1830 and 31, a number of them were collected on a reserve in the Township of Sarnia, near the head of the River St. Clair, and containing 10,280 acres. A number of houses were built for them, and an officer was appointed for their superintendence. Their conversion to christianity and their progress in religious knowledge, and in the acquisition of sober, orderly and industrious habits, have been under the care of Missionaries of the Wesleyan Methodist Society, both rapid and uniform. From the formation of the mission 221 adults and 239 children, have been baptized and admitted into the Methodist Community. The total number up to the year 1839–40, does not appear to have exceeded 350. Since then their number has increased greatly by immigration, chiefly from the Saginaw Bay, in the State of Michigan, and by the settlement of wandering Indians; and in 1842, as many as 741 received presents.

The Indians of the River aux Sables have about sixty acres under improvement, and one log house. Those at Kettle Point have twenty acres improved land and two log houses. The land on the Upper Reserve was regularly surveyed and laid out into farms. The Chief, with the approval of the Superintendent, placed most of the present occupants on these lands, but it is not indispensable that he should be consulted, as the members of the tribe may choose any unoccupied spot; when once in possession they are secure from intrusion, but repeated ill conduct or drunkenness would subject them to be expelled from the reserve of the Chief,

Wa-Wa-Nosh,
Salt. } *Chiefs*

4. Chippewas at Walpole Island

These Indians are also known under the name of Chippewas of Chenaille Ecarte. The Chippewas who have long hunted over the waste lands about the Chenaille Ecarte and Bear Creek, are a branch of the same nation which is settled in Sarnia, and share in the same annuity.

The Pottawatamies are recent immigrants from the United States.

The settlement at Walpole Island was commenced at the close of the American war, when Col. M'Kie, called by the Indians "White Elk," collected and placed upon the island which lies at the junction of the River and Lake St. Clair, the scattered remains of some tribes of Chippewas who had been engaged on the British side. Being left for many years without any interference or assistance on the part of the Government, they became a prey to the profligate whites settled on the frontier, who, by various frauds and in moments of intoxication, obtained leases and took possession of the most fertile and valuable part of the island.

5. Chippewas of the River Credit

These Indians are the remnant of a tribe which formerly possessed a considerable portion of the Home and Gore Districts, of which, in 1818, they surrendered the greater part, for an annuity of £532.10, reserving only certain small tracts at the River Credit, and at Sixteen and Twelve Mile Creeks. They were the first tribe converted to Christianity in Upper Canada.

Previous to the year 1823, they were wandering pagans. In that year, Messrs. Peter and John Jones, the sons of a white surveyor, and a Mississaga woman having been converted to Christianity, and admitted members of the Wesleyan Methodist Church, became anxious to redeem their countrymen from their degraded state of heathenism and destitution. They, accordingly, collected a considerable number together, and by rote and frequently repetitions, taught the first principles of Christianity to the adults, who were too far advanced in years to learn to read and write. In this manner the Lord's Prayer, the Creed, and the Commandments, were committed to memory. As soon as the tribes were converted, they perceived the evils attendant on their former state of ignorance and vagrancy. They began to work, which they never had done before; they recognized the advantage of cultivating the soil; they totally gave up drinking, to which they had been greatly addicted, and became sober, industrious, and consistent Christians.

J. SAWYER, } *Chiefs*
P. JONES, }

J. JONES, *War Chief*

6. THE CHIPPEWAS OF ALNWICK

These Indians were converted to Christianity in the years 1826–7. They were then pagans, wandering in the neighborhood of Belleville, Kingston, and Gananoque, and were known under the name of the Mississagas of the Bay of Quinte; in those years, between 200 and 300 were received into the Wesleyan Methodist Church, and settled on Grape Island, in the Bay of Quinte, six miles from Belleville, where they commenced planting, and where schools were established by the missionary for their instruction. On this island they resided eleven years, subsisting by agriculture and hunting. Their houses were erected partly by their own labor, and partly at the expense of the Methodist Missionary Society. The number, at length, amounted to twenty-three; besides which, they had a commodious building for religious service and schools, another room for an infant school, a hospital, a smithery, a shoemaker's shop, and a building for joiners' and cabinet work.

SUNDAY,
SIMPSON. } Chiefs

G. COMEGO, *Ch. & M. Inter.*

7. CHIPPEWAS AT RICE LAKE

These Indians belong to the same tribe, the Mississagas or Chippewas of Rice Lake, who in 1818, surrendered the greater part of the tract now forming the Newcastle District, for an annuity of £740. They have all been reclaimed from their primitive wandering life, and settled in their present locations within the last ten or twelve years.

The Rice Lake settlement is on the northern side of the lake, and at about twelve miles from Peterborough. The number of Indians is 114. They possess about 1550 acres of land, which are subdivided into 50 acre lots; of this, 1120 acres were granted in April, 1834, to trustees, "in trust, to hold the same for the benefit of the Indian tribes in the Province, and with a view to their conversion and civilization;" and the remaining 430 have been since purchased with their own funds. They have rather more land cleared than the Indians of Alnwick, about 400 acres; but the cultivation is not so good. The village contains thirty houses, three barns, a school-house, and a chapel with a bell. The Head Chief of the tribe resides here. For some time these Indians were under the charge of an officer appointed by the Indian Department, who assisted in their settlement; but at present they have no special Superintendent.

POUDASH,
COPWAY, } Chiefs
CROW.

8. CHIPPEWAS AT MUD LAKE

The Mud Lake Indians are settled on a point of land on the Mud or Chemong Lake, sixteen miles north-west of Peterborough. They are ninety-four in number, and possess twenty dwelling houses, with three stables. They occupy a grant of 1600 acres in the Township of Smith, made to the New England Company for their benefit, in April, 1837, of which about 200 acres are in cultivation. These Indians were for some time under the management of the late Mr. Scott, agent for the New England Company, and belong to the Wesleyan Methodist Church. A chapel is in the course of erection at the village, where there is already a mission house and a school.

NOGEE,
IRON, } *Chiefs*
MCKUE.

9. CHIPPEWAS AT BALSAM LAKE

The Balsam Lake Indians, ninety in number, are at present settled within the Township of Bexley, on a point of land jutting out into Lake Balsam, which is the most northerly of the chain of lakes, running northwest across the back Townships of the District of Newcastle. The Reserve which was granted to them by the Crown, is 1206 acres in extent. Of this they have about 200 acres in cultivation. Their village contains twelve houses, a barn, and a commodious school-house, in which divine service is performed by a resident Methodist missionary. But within the present year, (1843,) these Indians having become dissatisfied with the climate and the quality of the land at the Balsam Lake, have purchased six hundred acres on the banks of Lake Scugog, to be paid out of their share of their annuity, and are making preparations for removing from their former settlement. Their improvements will be sold for their benefit. Their reason for removing evinces their desire to advance in the pursuit of agriculture.

CRANE, *Chief*

10. CHIPPEWAS OF RAMA

These Indians formerly occupied the lands about Lake Simcoe, Holland River, and the unsettled country in the rear of the Home District. Genaral Darling reported of them in 1828, that they had expressed a strong desire to be admitted to Christianity, and to adopt the habits of civilized life; and that in these respects they might be classed with the Mississagas of the Bay of Quinte and Rice Lake, but were then in a more savage state. In 1830, Lieutenant-Governor Sir J. Colborne, collected them on a tract of land on the northwest shore of Lake Simcoe, of 9800 acres in extent, where they cleared a road between that lake and Lake Huron. They consisted of three tribes of Chippewas, under Chiefs Yellowhead, Aisance, and Snake, and a band of Pottiwatamies from Drummond Island; their number was about 500, under the care of Mr. Anderson, now the Superintendent at Manitoulin, who was appointed to take charge of their settlement and civilization; they made a rapid progress. The tribe under the Chief Yellow-head, now settled at Rama, were located at the Narrows on Lake Simcoe; Aisance's tribe, at present residing at Beausoleil, Matchadash Bay, was settled at Coldwater, at the other extremity of the Reserve, the distance between them being fourteen miles.

YELLOWHEAD,
NA-NAH-GE-SKUNG, } *Chiefs*
BIG SHILLINGE.

11. CHIPPEWAS OF BEAUSOLIEL ISLAND, MATCHADASH BAY, LAKE HURON

This band, under the chief "Aisance," is the same which was settled by Sir John Colborne, at Coldwater. Their present village, which is not very distant from the former settlement, was only commenced last year. It contains fourteen houses, and a barn: the number of the band is 232. They have about 100 acres under cultivation.

The majority of these Indians are Roman Catholics. They have not as yet any place of worship, or school. In the former settlement they were occasionally visited by the Roman Catholic priest, resident at Penetanguishene.

AISANCE, } *Chiefs*
JAMES KA-DAH-GE-QUON,

12. Chippewas of Snake Island, Lake Simcoe

This body of Indians was one of the three bands established at Cold water and the Narrows, and separated from them on the abandonment of those settlements. They now occupy one of the three Islands on Lake Simcoe, which were set apart for this tribe many years ago. They are 109 in number, and occupy twelve dwelling houses. They have also two barns and a school house, in which their children are instructed by a respectable teacher, and Divine Service is performed by a resident Missionary of the Methodist persuasion, to which these Indians belong. They have about 150 acres in cultivation, and are improving in habits of industry and agricultural skill. Their Missionary, who has been acquainted with them since July 1839, states that the majority of them are strictly moral in their character, that most of the adults are decidedly pious, and that many of them for consistency of character, would not suffer by a comparison with white christians of any denomination.

J. Snake, *Chief*

13. Chippewas of Saugeen, (Lake Huron.)

It was from these Indians, and their brethren, since settled at Owen's Sound, that Sir Francis Head, in 1836, obtained a surrender of the vast tract of land lying north of the London and Gore Districts, and between the Home District and Lake Huron, containing about 1,600,000 acres. He reserved at the same time, for the Indians, the extensive peninsula, lying between Lake Huron and Georgian Bay, north of Owen's Sound, and supposed to contain about 450,000 acres.

J. Metegoub,
Alexander, } *Chiefs*
Ah-Yah-Bance,

14. Chippewas of Big Bay, in Owen's Sound, Lake Huron

These Indians were formerly either wanderers in the Saugeen tract, surrendered to Sir F. Head, or live in scattered wigwams, on the shores of Big Bay. According to the agreement then made with them, it was proposed that they should either repair to Manitoulin or to that part of their former territory which lies north of Owen's Sound; upon which it was promised "that houses should be built for them, and proper assistance given, to enable them to become civilized, and to cultivate land."

JOHN JONES, } *Chiefs*
PETER, }

15. CHIPPEWAS AND OTHERS, IN THE TOWNSHIP OF BEDFORD.

Within a few years past, some stragglers from the Rice Lake tribe have settled in the Township of Bedford, about twenty-five miles north of the town of Kingston; and recently, they have been joined by a band of eighty-one Indians from Lower Canada, belonging to the post of the Lake of Two Mountains. As the settlement is of recent formation, and the claim of these Indians upon the attention of the Department of Upper Canada, has only been brought forward last year, they have not yet been visited by any officer of the Department, and no account can be given of the settlement. By Instructions issued in 1843, they were transferred from the Roll of Lower Canada to that of the Upper Province, and, accordingly, received their presents for the first time in that Province.

My beloved Reader—I am now about closing my narrative, and in doing this, there are but a few things to say. Throughout the work, I have confined my remarks chiefly to my own nation. But it must not be supposed, on this account, that I am forgetful of my brethren of the other Indian nations. The prayers and benevolent efforts of all Christendom should be directed towards all men every where. The gospel should be preached to every creature; and the field is the *wide* WORLD.

The Menomenees in Wisconsin, the Winebagoes and Potawatamees in Iowa, the warlike nations of the Sacs and Foxes, the Osages, Pawnees, Mandans, Kansas, Creeks, Omahas, Otoes, Delewares, Iowas, and a number of others elsewhere, must perish as did their brethren in the Eastern States, unless the white man send them the Gospel, and the blessings of education. There is field enough for all denominations to labor in, without interfering with each other. It is too late in the day to assert that the Indians cannot be raised up out of their degraded state, and educated for God and heaven. None need be discouraged since the Ojebwas in Western Canada have been converted. No language is adequate to portray the misery, wretchedness, and degradation in which we were, when the word of God was first brought and preached to us.

It is not necessary to detail each, and every wrong, that my poor people have suffered at the hands of the white man. Enough has already been said in various parts of the work, to prove that they have been most grossly abused, peeled, and wronged. Nor shall I notice the *personal wrongs* that I myself have received; and from those too, of whom I had good reason to hope better things. I once thought, that there were some things that I could never forgive; but the religion of Jesus, and the law of love, have taught me differently. I *do* forgive them; and may God forgive them and me too.

I have sometimes heard it said, that our forefathers were cruel to the forefathers of the whites. But was not this done through ignorance, or in self defense? Had your fathers adopted the plan of the great philanthropist, William Penn, neither fields, nor clubs, nor waters, would have been crimsoned with each others blood. The white men have been like the greedy lion, pouncing upon and devouring its prey. They have driven us from our nation, our homes, and possessions; compelled us to seek a refuge in Missouri, among strangers, and wild beasts; and will, perhaps, soon compel us to scale the Rocky Mountains; and, for aught I can tell, we may yet be driven to the Pacific Ocean, there to find our graves. My only trust is, that there is a just God. Was it to perpetrate such acts that you have been exalted above all other nations? Providence intended you for a *blessing* and not a *curse* to us. You have sent your missionaries to Burmah, China, the Sandwich Islands, and to almost every part of the world; and shall the Indians *perish at your own door?*

Is it not well known that the Indians have a generous and magnanimous heart? I feel proud to mention in this connection, the names of a Pocahontas, Massasoit, Skenandoah, Logan, Kusic, Pushmataha, Philip, Tecumseh, Osceola, Petalesharro, and thousands of others. Such names are an honor to the world! Let a late Governor of Massachusetts* speak for our fathers, when they first beheld the trembling white man:—

---

* Edward Everett. Esq.

"Brothers! when our fathers came over the great waters, they were a small band. The red man stood upon the rock by the seaside, and saw our fathers. He might have pushed them into the water and drowned them. But he stretched out his arm to our fathers and said, 'Welcome, white men!' Our fathers were hungry, and the red man gave them corn and venison. Our fathers were cold, and the red man wrapped them up in his blanket. We are now numerous and powerful, but we remember the kindness of the red man to our fathers."

And what have we received since, in return? Is it for the deeds of a Pocahontas, a Massasoit, and a host of others, that we have been plundered, and oppressed, and expelled from the hallowed graves of our ancestors? If help cannot be obtained from England and America, where else can we look? Will you then, lend us a helping hand; and make some amends for past injuries?

It is often said, that the Indians are *revengeful*, *cruel*, and *ungovernable*. But go to them with nothing but *the* BIBLE *in your hands*, and LOVE *in your hearts*, and you may live with them in perfect safety, share their morsel with them, and, like the celebrated Bartram, return to your homes UNHARMED. They very soon learn to venerate the Bible; as a proof of this, I will give an instance, that came under my own eye:—While at the Rabbit River Mission, a chief from the west, visited me. After reading to him several chapters from the Bible, he said, with much surprise, "Is *this* the book, that I hear so much about in *my* country?" I replied, yes; and these are the words of *Ke-sha-mon-e-doo* (the Great Spirit). "Will you not," said he, "give me one? I wish to show it to my people." I told him, not without you first promise that you will take care of it. He promised me that he would. I handed it to him; he took it, and turned it over and over; and then exclaimed, "*Wonderful, wonderful! this is the book of the Great Spirit!*" He then wrapped it up in a silk handkerchief, and the handkerchief in three or four folds of cloth. I heard, afterwards, from the trader, that the book was still kept sacred. O, if my poor brother could but *read* and *understand* that blessed volume, how soon would his dumb idols be "cast down to the moles and to the bats!" Will no one go and tell him and his nation, of the boundless, beseeching, bleeding, dying love of a Saviour; and urge upon them the importance of such a preparation of heart, as will enable them "to give up their account with joy?" The Great Spirit is no respecter of persons; He has made of one blood all the nations of the earth; He loves all his children alike; and his highest attributes are *love, mercy,* and *justice*. If this be so,—and who dare doubt it?—will He not stretch out his hand and help them, and avenge their wrongs? "If offences *must* come," let it be recollected, that *woe* is denounced against them "from *whom* they come."

I again propose that the territories of the Indians in the British dominions, be annexed to that Government, and those in the American dominions to the Federal Union. And, finally, in the language of that excellent, magnanimous, and benevolent friend of the poor children of the forest, Col. Thomas McKenney, I would say,

"I have already referred, in the commencement of this proposal to annex the Indian territory to our Union, to those good men, who, in the character of missionaries, have kept side by side with the Indians in so many of their afflictions and migrations. I will again refer to them, and implore them by all the lost labor of the past, and by the hopes of the future; by the critical condition of the pacific relations that exist between the Indians and us; and by the sacredness of the cause in which they are engaged, to look well and earnestly into this subject, and learn from the past what *must* attend upon their labors in the future, if the change I propose, or some other change equivalent to it, be not brought about. And, seeing, as they must see, that the plan I propose, or some other, is indispensable to the success they seek to command, I implore them to take up the subject in all its bearings, and by the instrumentalities which they have at command, manufacture, collect, and embody public opinion, in regard to what may be determined to be done; and by memorial, and personal agencies, bring this opinion to bear upon Congress, with whom alone the power is vested, to redeem, disenthrall, and save, and bless, the remnants of this aboriginal race. And I make the same appeal to all the good, of all religious persuasions, both in the Church and out of it, and politicians of all parties, to second this attempt, feeble as I know it to be, to save the Indians, and consolidate, and perpetuate peace between them and us, and by so doing, ward off the terrible retribution which must sooner or later, unless it be averted, fall upon this nation."

A Note About the Author

George Copway (1818–1869) was a Mississauga Ojibwa writer, missionary, and advocate. Born in Trenton, Ontario, his Ojibwa name was Kah-ge-ga-gah-Bowh, meaning He Who Stands Forever. His father John was a medicine man and Mississauga chief who converted to Methodism in 1827. Sent to a nearby mission school, Copway became a missionary in 1834, working in Wisconsin to translate the Book of Acts and the Gospel of St Luke into Ojibwa. After earning an appointment as a Methodist minister, Copway moved with his wife to Minnesota, where they would raise a son and daughter while serving as missionaries. In 1846, accusations of embezzlement for his work on the Ojibwe General Council forced him to leave the Methodist church. The next year, he published *The Life, History, and Travels of Kah-Ge-Ga-Gah-Bowh*, a bestselling memoir that was the first book published by a Canadian First Nations writer. Encouraged by this success, Copway launched a weekly New York City newspaper called *Copway's American Indian* but failed to keep his venture afloat despite letters of support from Lewis Henry Morgan, James Fenimore Cooper, and Washington Irving. Over the next decade, he succumbed to alcoholism and debt, and was left by his wife and daughter in 1858. Copway spent the last years of his life writing on Indian history, working as an herbalist, and recruiting troops for the Union army.

A Note from the Publisher

CPSIA information can be obtained
at www.ICGtesting.com
Printed in the USA
LVHW021928130521
687357LV00014B/1289